The Dubliner 100 Best Restaurants 2012
Compiled by Martha Connolly, Katie Byrne, Louise Finn,
paul trainer, Lauren Hisada, Caitríona McBride, Bridget
Hourican, Victoria Mary Clarke & Paddy Cullivan
Design by Ciara McLoughlin
Additional research by Jason O'Sullivan & Caroline Gleeson
Photography by Robert McCann

Thanks to gleesons incorporating gilbeys

# The Dubliner

First edition, published November 2011
isbn 978-0-9570894-0-2
*The Dubliner* magazine,
3 Ely Place, Dublin 2, Ireland.
t: (01) 480 4700. editor@thedubliner.ie.
www.thedubliner.ie

## NOTE ON PRICING
All dinner and lunch price are *à la carte*. Please check with the restaurants for any early birds, tasting menus or specials available.

Santa *Rita*
RESERVA

SINCE 1880

CABERNET SAU
D.O. VALLE DEL MAIPO -

# FOREWORD

Santa Rita, the leading Chilean wine in Ireland, is delighted to be associated once again with *The Dubliner 100 Best Restaurants* for the tenth year running.

At Santa Rita, we have a global reputation for producing some of the world's most heavenly wines. From our best known brand within the portfolio, Santa Rita 120, our extensive range of award-winning Reserva wines to our Icon wine Casa Real, we have a wine to suit every taste and budget.

As we look forward to the year ahead, it's fantastic to see that restaurants are doing a wonderful job of providing customers with extensive and innovative menu options as well as offering great value for money. At Santa Rita, we are delighted to be in a position to recognise and reward this ongoing innovation and creativity in the sector.

The Santa Rita People's Choice Award continues to be the jewel in the crown for Dublin restaurants, as it is voted by you the public – the toughest critics of all! So pour yourself a glass of Ireland's favourite Chilean wine, Santa Rita, and join us in congratulating the 100 best restaurants in Dublin for 2012.

SALLY-ANNE COONEY
*General Manager*
*Gleesons incorporating Gilbeys*

# INTRODUCTION

Congratulations to Pichet, winner of our Santa Rita People's Choice Award, as voted by you, our readers. The results come directly from over 2,500 people who filled out the voting form we printed in *The Dubliner* each Thursday with the *Evening Herald*.

Pichet was the clear favourite, and deservedly so. The combination of head chef Stephen Gibson's wonderful food and front of house Nick Munier's inimitable hospitality is most certainly a winning one, and we at *The Dubliner* wish the two and their hard-working team continued success.

In this, our tenth edition of *The Dubliner 100 Best Restaurants*, I would also like to extend my warmest appreciation to our readers, our sponsor Santa Rita and our team of reviewers.

MARTHA CONNOLLY
*Editor, The Dubliner*

4, St. Andrew Street,
Dublin 2.

Tel: 677 5545

**PRICES:**
- Starters €5.71-€9.56
- Mains €15.36-€30.93
- House Wine: €21

**OPENING:**
Mon-Sat from 4.30pm

www.trocadero.ie

# 10. THE TROCADERO

The name's rococo and so's the interior: all red velvet, cushy banquettes, signed photos, brass fittings, marble fireplaces, glass lampshades, gilt mirrors, art deco bar, mosaic pillars... The buzz never falls below excitable and you'll find that every time you come back, it always feels like the first night.

Actually, the Troc is the wrong side of the river for the major theatres, but it's still the theatre restaurant *par excellence*. Great theatrical names gaze down from the walls – and lesser ones turn round from the bar to see who's coming in. There's probably nowhere better for large groups, or first dates if you don't know whether you'll get on. There's a lot of fodder for good conversation and if that fails, you can always start people-watching.

The ambience is so warm it would heat up Alaska and maitre d' Robert Doggett makes everyone feel like they've just won an Oscar. Waiters are old-school and twinkly-eyed – it's visible that they're happy to be there and what a difference that makes to a dining experience. If we're going to be honest, we have to say that nobody comes for the food really, but the food is just fine. The fried brie (€8.16) is a bit of a signature starter.

The mains count four fish dishes and three different kinds of steaks, plus three vegetarian options. This includes their trademark cannellini (€19), which is made by Robert's sister. You shouldn't confuse this with their cannelloni (€17.29), though it's also delicious with scrolls of fresh pasta filled with beef and spinach. Get close to the bone, if you wish, with their T-bone (€28.81) or grilled sole on the bone (€28.62).

Of course they do a pre-theatre menu from 5pm, but you really want to be here after hours, with all the time in the world to spare. The Troc is a Dublin institution, one of the city's longest-running restaurants, and it shows. You don't get this charm and patina except with age.

> 66
> *Robert Doggett is Dublin's most charming man.*
> 99
>
> Sarah Tolan

**SIGNATURE DISH**

*Chargrilled fillet steak.*
*€30.73*

> 66
> *They don't make them like The Troc any more.*
> 99
>
> Sophie Taylor

**BOOKING:** Tel: *677 5545, email trocaderoireland @gmail.com*

# 9. SABA

26-28 Clarendon St,
Dublin 2.
Tel: 679 2000

**PRICES:**
- Starters €2.85-12.45
- Mains €13-24
- House Wine: €19.50

**OPENING:**
Mon-Sun lunch & dinner
www.sabadublin.com

S aba is an oxymoron. Upmarket fast food? It's a paradox as well, as the chefs come straight from Thailand, but Saba doesn't aim for – and you don't get – a particularly authentic South Asian experience. So this inevitably produces that larger question in the collective mind of the clientele: is the focus on the glitz or is it on the food? And are those decibels really conducive to eating? Our readers agree that the answer to this is both, with the two elements working together in near perfect harmony.

We imagine it's tough, but it's obviously working for Saba to shunt between the extremes of East/West, dining/partying, posh nosh and fast food. To put it plainly, it works.

Now, it especially works if you're in a large group of girls – maybe a hen party – looking to blow your week's wages on cocktails. But if this isn't the case and your preoccupation is solely the food – light, zesty, Asian fusion food, to be specific – you're more than safe here. Paul Cadden believes in great value for money and he's delivering it with his beautiful, satisfyingly portioned arrangements for reasonable prices. Their hake in banana leaf with a red curry sauce (€16.95) is particularly eye-catching as it arrives in a steaming boat topped with basil and a spectrum of peppers.

For a light starter, try their tempura pak: crisp, delicately battered veg with a mustard lime mayonnaise (€7.60). Everything feels fresh and tangy and the hand on the fish sauce isn't too heavy. We're addicted to the hoisin duck rolls (€8.15), the meing kam (€9.95) and the beef marinated in beer with ginger and soya sauce.

With Saba's hip decor in black lacquered tables, fuchsia table mats and patterned wooden dividers, its enticing bamboo steam baskets, bang-on city location and its ever-milling crowds, it's a fun, consistent and cosmopolitan establishment in these changing times.

> **So much fun. We always end up back here.**
>
> Catherine Burton

### SIGNATURE DISH

*Hake wrapped in a banana leaf served with a red curry sauce.* €20.15

> **The best Thai food in Dublin. A great place to eat.**
>
> Anthony O'Grady

**BOOKING:**
Tel: 679 2000
www.sabadublin.ie

23 Upper Pembroke
Street, Dublin 2.
Tel: 676 1494

**PRICES:**
- Starters: €10-18
- Mains: €18-33
- House Wine: €30

**OPENING:**
Lunch: Tues-Fri
Dinner: Tues-Sat

www.dax.ie

# 8. DAX

Come over to Dax this autumn – well come all year round, but you owe it to yourself to be here for game season. You won't find a better roast partridge (with sumptuous curried butternut squash puree, confit potatoes, glazed shallot and prune juice for €27), venison (€28) or wood pigeon (€14) – all served with a delicious sweet glazed jus. Dax takes eating and service very seriously – in the good old-fashioned French way.

Yes, the prices are quite serious, so unless you've managed to float and keep your head above these recessionary waters, it might be a place for special occasions (unless the girl of your dreams has finally agreed to let you take her on a date), but the emphasis here is on the experience: once you're within their doors they do everything to make your time memorable. Last time we went for lunch and ordered just one main each, with water – they brought a load of amuse bouches for free. No wonder it's a fave with the media-politico-muso crowds.

The location, Pembroke Street, just up from Fitzwilliam Square, is discreet and so is the dining room, a cosy, swanky, white-washed basement. But for the absolute perfect experience, chef Olivier Meisonnave has to be there. Going to Dax without being welcomed by the quietly charismatic ex-rugby player is a bit like watching *The Late Late* without Gay Byrne – the essence, or *raison d'etre* is missing. Fortunately, Olivier is generally in situ, exuding reassurance and bonhomie, and offering advice on the wine list – he used to be sommelier in Thornton's. Do take his advice – the wine list runs to 20 pages and ranges from about €25 a bottle to €400. It's not all French – though don't look for the New World; that would be going too far. The name Dax, in case you're wondering, comes from a spa town in the Aquitaine region of southwest France. Trust us, it's more appropriate than you could initially imagine.

**SIGNATURE DISH**

*Roast partridge with curried butternut squash puree, confit potatoes, glazed shallots and a prune jus. €27*

**BOOKING:**
Tel: 676 1494
*www.dax.ie*

# 7. JO'BURGER

137 Rathmines Road,
Dublin 6.

Tel: 491 3731

**PRICES:**
- Starters: €5
- Mains: €8.95-12.50
- House Wine: €18.50

**OPENING:**
Mon-Sun lunch & dinner

www.joburger.ie

A former winner of the Santa Rita People's Choice Award, Jo'Burger remains a hit with Dubliners who queue for a spot on the long communal tables of this small, quirky burger bar. When you arrive, you'll probably notice that the music is a bit too loud, the graffiti décor is bang-on-trend and the staff are trendy. The room looks like your typical hipster hangout, but the food has made this a regular destination for the broadest range of diners imaginable. They're all here – awkward new couples, parents and their fidgety kids, matronly ladies, broad-shouldered jocks, culchie blow-ins, collections of middle-aged friends trying to catch the waitress' eye to order more wine. The enduring appeal of the lamb, fish, chicken, beef and veggie burger-based menu is quite remarkable. Much credit is due to Joe Macken, the rakish, colourful restaurateur whose commitment to big flavours and unusual ingredients is the basis of everything that is right about this place.

A Macken side-project, CrackBird – a pop-up restaurant serving up a chicken in a variety of guises – has been one of the culinary smash hits of the year and is expected to soon find a permanent home, and we hear there will be a new city centre venue for Jo'Burger in the new year too. Whether this will mean the end for their original Rathmines location is unclear. We hope they remain, particularly due to their sensational food delivery service that is guaranteed to provide mealtime happiness for Southsiders enjoying a lazy weekend.

Recently, the original menu has been augmented with regular experimental burgers and sides, so look out for combinations involving the likes of twice cooked pears, chilli thyme honey, roasted chorizo and portions of unusual sounding croquettes. When we visit, we order a Zola beef burger stacked with roast pepper, rocket and almond pesto served on a huge Breton roll (€11.50) and ask for a portion of sweet potato fries (€4.95). Quite frankly, delicious.

> 66
> *Jo'Burger is the perfect hangover cure.*
> 99
>
> Simon Sweeney

## SIGNATURE DISH

*The Zola beef burger; a Jo' burger served with roast pepper and rocket almond pesto. €11.50*

> 66
> *Cool vibe and awesome burgers.*
> 99
>
> Olivia Burke

**BOOKING:**
No reservations

47 Ranelagh Village,
Dublin 6.
Tel: 497 8010

**PRICES:**
- Starters: €4.50-11.50
- Mains: €12.50-26
- House Wine: €22

**OPENING:**
Lunch: Fri-Sun
Dinner: Mon-Sun

www.dillingers.ie

# 6. DILLINGER'S

Ranelagh Village is equipped with an embarrassment of riches when it comes to restaurants. This is undoubtedly Dublin's most popular dining strip, and Dillinger's is part of the young up-and-coming pack of fashionable bistros that currently has the chattering classes working themselves into a lather. The menu is part posh New York diner, part classic grill-house. We particularly love the few nods to the joyous experience that is classic North American indulgence. Nachos grande with a mountain of Texas bbq chilli beef and beans, avocado, cheese, sour cream and jalapenos for €15! The inimitable corn dogs – beer-battered smoked franks served with cheddar cheese fondue and sauerkraut for €14! For those who find these meat delights distasteful there is an excellent selection of vegetarian dishes designed by Denis Cotter of Café Paradiso fame. The papardelle in lemon cream with puy lentils, red onion and panfried artichokes (€16) is both pretty and tasty. For those who don't mind dining out at off-peak times of the week, there is a Happy Hour (and a bit) on Tuesday and Wednesday offering all alcoholic drinks ordered between 5.30pm and 6.45pm at half-price. On Monday nights you can start the week here with a veritable all-American feast of Southern fried chicken, smoky baked beans, coleslaw and a large helping of fries for €14. When John Farrell teamed up with Temple Garner, formerly of Town Bar and Grill (Garner has since left, and been replaced by new head chef Ross Morgan), to come up with the idea for Dillinger's, they were by no means sure of success.

The popularity of this venue over the last two years encouraged the pair to open The Butcher's Grill, which serves up Desperate Dan-size hunks of meat and mouthwatering sides just across the road. The new year will see them branch out again with the ridiculously named 777 Mexican restaurant on George's Street.

> **A really good, buzzy atmosphere.**
>
> Keith Foley

**SIGNATURE DISH**

*Lemon and tarragon marinated free-range rotisserie chicken with maple-glazed sweet potato chips and corn on the cob. €21*

> **My fave place for brunch.**
>
> Olivia Burke

BOOKING:
497 8010
info@dillingers.ie

# 5. EATERY 120

120 Ranelagh Road,
Dublin 6.
Tel: 470 4120

**PRICES:**
- Starters: €5.75-9.75
- Mains: €14.50-27
- House Wine: €20

**OPENING:**
Lunch: Fri-Sun
Dinner: Mon-Sun

*www.eatery120.ie*

Eatery 120 is arguably the most genuinely neighbourhood of all the 'neighbourhood' restaurants in Ranelagh, in that it's consistent in quality, value, and you can probably walk in and get a table midweek (but book weekends). They've recently done a Fallon & Byrne downstairs – i.e opened a wine bar called (you guessed it) Winery 120 – that serves small plates, charcuterie and cheese, but if you're coming for dinner, try and get a table upstairs in the library nook. The options on the menu are as you'd expect for a neighbourhood place – the ubiquitous burger, beer-batter fish 'n' chips, pork belly, rib-eye steak – but it's all cooked with a light touch and served with casual grace. The Eatery burger (€15.50-18.95) is hard to turn down as it's served with the enticing option of bacon and Cashel blue cheese; and the slow-cooked belly of pork with apple and smoked bacon sauerkraut, whipped mash and wholegrain mustard (€21.25) is also a strong favourite.

Chef Eoin Costelloe, has some magnificent signature menu highlights, which include the mushrooms on toast with tarragon cream (€7.75) and the sweet potato and chickpea stew with brown rice (€14), which make a healthier and more wholesome veggie option than you'll find in many places. The mid-week menu (two courses for €20) means you can have the best of both worlds, and its popularity would suggest that many people regularly do.

But the *raison d'etre* of a place like this is weekend brunch – and sure enough you'll be hard put to find a seat after 10am as hungover Ranelagh denizens take their free-range poached eggs, buttermilk pancakes, and, of course, bloody Marys, very seriously. These happy patrons can often be viewed sitting in the floor-to-ceiling window enjoying their meal and engaging in an intense session of people-watching. The location of this restaurant means that if you get the right seat, you'll feel like the world is at your fingertips.

> **“**
> *I always look forward to having dinner here.*
> **”**
>
> Declan McCourt

### SIGNATURE DISH

*Pan roast cod with spinach, samphire, palourde clams, black olive gnocchi and a velouté sauce. €21.75*

> **“**
> *The staff are so friendly. They get it right every time.*
> **”**
>
> Nuala Lynch

BOOKING:
470 4120
eat@eatery120.ie

18-19 Parnell Square,
Dublin 1.
Tel: 873 2266

**SET MENUS:**
● Lunch: 3-course €36.50
● Pre-theatre: €36.50
● Dinner: €65

**OPENING:**
Lunch: Tues-Fri
Dinner: Tues-Sat

www.chapteronerestaurant.com

# 4. CHAPTER ONE

What can we say? At the risk of sounding like a stuck record, we'll offer that Chapter One is still keeping up those impeccable standards (and that we're still really into that Chef's Table made out of volcanic rock). All around the city, establishments, institutions and people may be cutting their cloth to suit this year's fashion, but Chapter One continues to steer its trademark steady course between fine dining, wonderful service and a relaxed, unstuffy atmosphere. Well, if it ain't broke, don't fix it, right? Owner Ross Lewis is still in the kitchen, still gently pushing the boundaries. His poached cod with lobster, artichoke and spider crab mayonnaise is the perfect example of a dish that's daring without making any sudden, alarming or pretentious moves. He lets the flavours, which come from local artisan suppliers, speak for themselves – and they certainly do.

The portions for this type of Michelin-starred food are pretty generous, so you'll get to spend some significant time with them (the flavours, that is). Like a gastronomic version of De Valera, Ross seems to be able to look into his stomach and know what the Irish people will eat. The fact that at a fee you can see your decadent meal cooked and explained to you in careful detail further means that Ross knows how to appeal to his clientele. And it has to be said that the welcome at Chapter One is still probably the best in Dublin. We know of one woman who turned up pretty late and furious with her prevaricating husband. Instead of intentionally making her feel guilty for keeping the table waiting (which some restaurant staff have been known to do), the staff soothingly accommodated her. Within minutes her rage evaporated.

The only churlish remark we've ever heard on Chapter One is that the rich, Southside clientele are over-compensating for their daring in venturing north of the Liffey – but we think that just shows a partionist mindset.

> **"**
> *Unbelievably good food.*
> **"**
>
> Melanie Costello

### SIGNATURE DISH

*Dombes duck breast with fried cabbage and smoked potato, carrot and black cumin puree in a sauce sharpened with apple balsamic vinegar. (Set Menu)*

> **"**
> *Fantastic service. It really makes for a night to remember.*
> **"**
>
> Alan Fitzsimons

*BOOKING:*
*873 2266. info@ chapteronerestaurant.com*

**PEOPLE'S CHOICE AWARD TOP 10**

# 3. JUNIORS

2 Bath Avenue,
Dublin 4.

Tel: 664 3648

**PRICES:**
- Starters: €5-9
- Mains: €16-24
- House Wine: €20

**OPENING:**
Lunch: Mon-Sat
Dinner: Mon-Sat

*www.juniors.ie*

**D**on't be expecting a Versailles-style dining space here, but don't let the small size put you off either. Once you are prepared for the cramped tables (do not play accidental footsie with diners next to you, we did and learnt that people will inevitably get the wrong idea), Juniors is a joy, always full and buzzing. Expect to wait for a table, but this is the perfect opportunity to nip in to Slattery's pub for a quick pint around the corner. Besides, the creative and consistent food is well worth the wait.

Try to resist their juicy pint o' prawns

with toast and homemade mayo at €9, while lunch attracts punters like moths to the flame for their huge and delicious NYC-style sandwiches. The conversant and friendly waiting staff, who sure know how to sell a dish, made us go for the starter of grilled peaches with buffalo mozzarella, walnut pesto and rocket (€8). They really shouldn't be forcing such things on people, as it'll end in their own loss (It was so good we've been cheekily passing it off as our own creation at dinner parties). Their crab linguini with chilli, parsley, garlic and olive oil (€18) is as rich as it is meaty and their sausage and mash with red onion relish (€15) adds to the pure comfort of the place.

A dessert of homemade marshmallows (€6) – when done well (which they do) – is also hopelessly enticing. Now, if you're waiting to hear how they take comfort to the next level (steady now, those of you with vivid imaginations), read on. It just so happens that if you are sitting outside and are feeling a bit chilly, the staff at Junior's will provide you with a selection of snug fleece blankets and even hot water bottles. Like you're at a pal's house, right? A very accommodating pal, perhaps... Even Darina Allen has been spotted dining here – quite the seal of approval.

> **"**
> *This is the coolest little restaurant in Dublin.*
> **"**
>
> Eve Horgan

**SIGNATURE DISH**

*Chargrilled chicken sandwich with slow roasted tomatoes, lemon and basil aioli, rocket and roast tomatoes. €6*

> **"**
> *I live here at the weekend.*
> **"**
>
> Caroline Saunders

BOOKING:
Call in on the day

3-5 Exchequer Street,
Dublin 2.
Tel: 670 6787

**PRICES:**
● Starters: €3.95-19.95
● Mains: €14.95-21.95
● House Wine: €22

**OPENING:**
Lunch: Mon-Sun
Dinner: Mon-Sun

*www.theexchequer.ie*

# 2. THE EXCHEQUER

Much of the cool energy of South William Street and its strip of hip hangouts trickled down towards the top of Dame Lane around two years ago when this self-styled gastro pub opened its doors. Readers of *The Dubliner* have been charmed by the ambitious menu making this one of the leading venues for casual dining in the city centre.

The food has been overshadowed in some ways by the bar's reputation as the place to be for rugby players, visiting musicians, dazzling media celebrities and a steady stream of models and arty types. Don't let that put you off. Decent people eat and drink here too. Their success is more remarkable considering The Exchequer was shoe-horned into the side of the ancient Central Hotel – whose most recent celebrity diner was Michael Collins. A starter platter here is a joy to behold. On our last visit we were presented with a long wooden board laden with a foie gras and duck liver parfait, partnered with apple chutney and a couple of wedges of toasted brioche; beignet of goats' cheese with a beetroot purée and calamari with a citrus salad (€10).

Our knives were immediately in the 'en guard' position, ready to fend off any fork aiming for the choicest part of the entrees. The calamari and the goats' cheese were beautifully prepared and rich in flavour, but the star of the show was foie gras parfait – a real treat. We could happily gorge ourselves on pints of this stuff if they had it on draft behind the bar. It's that good. We also enjoy the cherry-smoked bacon and cabbage with a mustard, spring onion, cheddar cheese and potato croquette, sweet potato purée, black pudding and apple chutney (€19.95).

The menu changes regularly so we look forward to sampling the treats that Ian Tucker, Peter Rock and their team have in store for us in the year ahead. Honourable mention to their cocktail list, arguably the most innovative in the city.

> **Their Sunday roast is amazing.**
>
> *David O'Neill*

### SIGNATURE DISH

*Cherry-smoked bacon and cabbage with a mustard, spring onion and cheddar cheese potato croquette, sweet potato puree, black pudding and apple chutney. €19.95*

> **Really popular. Trendy, yet unpretentious.**
>
> *Jane Murphy*

BOOKING:
670 6787
info@theexchequer.ie

14-15 Trinity Street,
Dublin 2.
Tel: 677 1060

**PRICES:**
- Starters: €6-16
- Mains €19-28
- House Wine: €22.50

**OPENING:**
Lunch: Mon-Sun
Dinner: Mon-Sun

www.pichetrestaurant.com

# 1. PICHET

The room's a slightly awkward L-shape
– the result of soldering together two
former establishments, a pasta bar
and a café. The music can be loud and veer
towards Spin FM. But do these things
matter? Nope. Everyone involved with
Pichet is having a lot of fun.

Remember the Michelin Parisian chef
who turned in his stars and said he was
opening a bistro because he wanted to
let loose? That's the vibe you'll get when
you're in Pichet. The owners' pedigrees
are gastronomically impeccable – chef
Stephen Gibson is from l'Ecrivain and
front-of-house Nick Munier comes via the
Roux brothers, the K Club and Patrick
Guilbaud. But they've left behind the

hushed atmospheres while managing to keep the fine dining. The food here is full of imagination and free of fuss. We'll wager the biggest fuss you'll have while you're here is in trying to figure out what starter to order – it's pretty impossible to choose. The crispy fried lamb with chickpeas and harissa mayonnaise (€10) is rich and tangy, and the Castletownbere crab and mussels on sourdough (€12) will leave you feeling warm and content.

If you wanted to take two and skip the mains you'd undoubtedly be satisfied. However, it would be a damn shame to not try their impossibly tender suckling pig with puy lentils, Toulouse sausage, sauerkraut and wholegrain mustard (€20). The dessert menu benefits from a stroke of genius, as well, with the option to order just three petit fours. This for when you're experiencing that familiar conundrum in which you can't face death by chocolate but really, really want something sweet. Are we projecting? The clientele are very on-the-town: people with exciting lives perch on the wonderful Pan Am blue leather chairs, shouting their recent peccadillos across to each other.

Of course, it helps that Nick's never off the telly (*Hell's Kitchen*, *Masterchef Ireland*), and that diners feel they're participating in a fly-on-the-wall documentary. A most deserving winner of the Santa Rita People's Choice Award.

> 66
> *The food here is just gorgeous.*
> 99
>
> Amy O'Loughlin

**SIGNATURE DISH**

*A crispy hen's egg with Serrano ham, baby leeks and caper vinaigrette. €9.50*

> 66
> *Pichet is so special, my first choice in Dublin.*
> 99
>
> Niamh O'Dowd

BOOKING:
677 1060
info@pichetrestaurant.com

25 ∎

SEE P77

## Chef's Chef Award

And the Santa Rita Chef's Chef Award 2012 goes to ...

# DERRY CLARKE

*of L'Ecrivain*

**We asked chefs and restaurateurs** from our 100 Best list to tell us who is the best chef right now. Dubliner Derry Clarke topped the poll to be hailed by his peers as the Santa Rita Chef's Chef 2012. After 22 years in business, Derry and wife Sallyanne Clarke are restaurant royalty in this town. Legend has it that on the day the money-men from the IMF rolled into Dublin, they were shocked to arrive for dinner in L'Ecrivain to find it positively rocking on a Monday night. Proof positive that Derry Clarke is a man for all seasons and that our longest-standing Michelin-starred establishment has a warm place in our hearts.

## AND THE HONOURABLE MENTIONS

Ross Lewis, *Chapter One*

Kevin Thornton, *Thornton's*

Padraic Hayden, *Camden Kitchen*

Dylan McGrath, *Rustic Stone*

# ANANDA

Dundrum Town Centre,
Sandyford Road,
Dublin 14

*www.anandarestaurant.ie*

**P**ut aside any preconceptions you have about Indian food, as a visit to Ananda will undoubtedly revise your opinion. The menu is a marriage of Indian flavours and the finest of Irish produce – as fusion cuisine goes, it's certainly the most imaginative available in Dublin. Signature dishes include Lobster Xec-Xec: pan-fried Howth lobster in a classic Goan-style sauce with chutney pulao (€34.50) and 18-hour marinated Fermanagh rare breed black pork chop with vindaloo masala and coastal red rice (€21.50). The menu is devised by Atul Kochhar (the first Indian chef to receive a Michelin star in the UK) and created by Sunil Ghai, a chef whose bibs have been decorated with countless shiny medals. Ananda is housed in the cinema building in Dundrum Town Centre, but the unusual location doesn't upset the overall ambience. The

- Starters: €7.50- €15
- Mains: €16.50- €33.50
- House Wine: €22

OPENING: Lunch: Fri-Sun
Dinner: Mon-Sun

décor is stylish and intimate, with art deco string door curtains dividing the space, striking lighting features and pops of vivid colour. The service – friendly and attentive – is equally noteworthy. For good value, check out the early bird special: €20 for two courses (Sunday-Friday 5:30pm-7pm and Saturday 5:30pm-6:30pm). A recent redecoration includes a new cocktail lounge where they do a dangerously good Caipirinha. We're just saying...

**BOOKING:** Tel: 296 0099, email: info@ananda.ie

■ 28

# ANDERSONS CREPERIE

1A Carlingford Road,
Drumcondra, Dublin 9.
www.andersons.ie

Let's talk about crepes (baby). Yes, Andersons do sandwiches and lots of other nice things, but the main attraction is what keeps the hordes coming. If your idea of a pancake is the kind of burnt, lemon and siucra-sprinkled offering your mam wheels out before Lent, then you need to go here to be reeducated, as owners Noel Delaney and Patricia Van der Velde take the art of crepe-making very seriously. Here, there's something for every type of tooth, the sweet and the savoury. For the former, the pavlova crepe (€7.95) comes highly recommended, and for the latter, the all-day breakfast galette is our poison of choice (€9.65). We're not sure which we prefer, but one thing is for certain, it's one or the other as these are belly-busting affairs. Andersons gets very busy at the weekend, so either get there early or arrive later and be prepared for a bit of a wait. On Friday nights they have live jazz sessions, which make this the perfect time to take a beloved there and impress them. Be warned that they are very child friendly – they have a dedicated kids menu – so if you're nursing a hangover, this is not the spot for you.

- Starters: €7.95-9.95
- Mains: €7.95-11.50
- House Wine: €18

OPENING: Lunch: Mon-Sun
Dinner: Fri-Sat

**BOOKING:** Tel: 830 5171

# AVOCA

**11-13 Suffolk Street,
Dublin 2.**

*www.avoca.ie*

**W**hen you walk into Avoca on Suffolk Street, you're stuck with a terrible dilemma – upstairs or downstairs? The brain melts. Upstairs on the first floor is the main restaurant, a favourite haunt of the Dublin yummy mummy who likes to take little Oscar and Poppy (or whatever these people are calling their kids these days) out for a bite in the afternoon after yoga. Yes, it is terribly middle class, and yes it is rather irritating, but we are willing to put up with it for the sake of the food. Try the Clare Island salmon cakes (€13.95) if you fancy tasting a little bit of heaven. Also, just FYI, the waiters are very easy on the eye here, which is another sweetener. Plus, and here's the kicker, they've recently refurbished the basement, so if you decide to go downstairs you can avail of their more relaxed sambo, cake and takeaway menu, which you can enjoy at their newly installed seating. It's slightly more laid-back, with fewer on-trend buggies. The choice is yours. We hasten to add that both get very busy at the weekends and going into Avoca always puts you at risk of succumbing to a knick-knack and woollen blanket, impulse-buying frenzy. You have been warned.

- Starters: €5.50-8
- Mains: €14-16
- House Wine: €20

**OPENING:** Mon-Sat, 9.30pm - 5pm. Sunday 11am-5.30pm

---

**BOOKING:** Tel: 672 6019

# THE BAKE HOUSE

6 Bachelors Walk,
Dublin 2.
www.the-bakehouse.ie

**NEW ENTRY**

**C**an you believe that it is 10 years since RTÉ screened the first episode of *Bachelors Walk*? If the same programme was made today, it would be set in a different city. This little section of the quays remains lively, and we made our first visit to The Bakehouse on one of the last sunny evenings of the year. A reader had informed us they serve the best sandwiches in Dublin. We're not ready to go that far – yet – but The Bakehouse selection is impressive. We had a bloomer stuffed with succulent pieces of pork belly, layered with caramelised apples and lathered with wholegrain mustard (€12.95) – a full meal rather than a snack, served with a side of spuds, so don't gasp too hard at the price. Our companion opted for a delicious chicken and vegetable pie served with mash (€9.50). As you can tell, the menu leans heavily towards the traditional and hearty dishes. They also have some salads if you are into that kind of thing. The staff did well to serve a small but busy room. They even managed the occasional smile. Whether you are visiting for lunch or dinner we recommend you linger a while and people watch over a bottle of Keenan's Bridge Cabernet Shiraz (€19).

- Starters: €4.50-9.50
- Mains: €5.20-13.95
- House Wine: €19

OPENING: **Lunch:** Mon-Sun
**Dinner:** Thurs-Sat

**BOOKING:** Tel: 873 4279

# BERNARD SHAW

11-12 South
Richmond Street,
Dublin 2.

The *Dubliner* has enthused in a giddy manner about the hedonistic nocturnal delights of The Bernard Shaw. In the cold light of day though, in the absence of beats and Buckfast, without the presence of outlandishly dressed pretty young things, we are faced with the stark reality: this is an old pub marooned on a dingy corner. However, somehow this daytime image has been completely transformed by Italians Leandro Virgilio and Daria Santilli. They have lovingly crafted a vibrant, comfortable enclave in this most unlikely of edifices. They call this daytime construction Coffee To Get Her, a neat little title for their makeshift café and a declaration of intent. Not long after the last lank-haired scamp has shuffled off the dancefloor the night before, this pair are serving breakfast and fresh coffee in the front room. You'll find parents sipping espresso and their little ones snacking on Italian croissants. At lunchtime we love the Arrosticini platter of handmade lamb skewers made on a specially imported Rosticcio gas grill, served with salad and garlic bread. Prepared with love, packed with flavour and one of this town's genuine bargains at €7.50. Perfect with a glass of Montepulciano d'Abruzzo (€4) served by passionate, charming staff. An unexpectedly satisfying lunch venue.

● Mains: €7-10
● Wine: €4 per glass

OPENING: Lunch: Mon-Sat

**BOOKING:** No reservations, but telephone 085 712 8342

# BIBI'S

14b Emorville Avenue,
South Circular Road,
Dublin 8.
www.bibis.ie

**B**ibi's describes itself as "cosy but cosmopolitan". This translates as tiny but popular with people who wish they lived in Greenwich Village, or at least Shoreditch. Despite the limited space and the occasional diner partial to wearing Wayfarer sunglasses indoors, this boutique café is utterly adorable. Hidden on a sleepy Portobello street, the outside terrace is occupied by fashionable locals in decent weather. Inside there are a few tables lined up opposite a counter adorned with spectacular cakes. Specials of the day are scribbled on a chalkboard. One of the most popular items are Turkish eggs – poached eggs on toast with spiced butter and natural yoghurt (€8.95). It is possible to accessorise before or after your meal in the adjoining Doll's Boutique, a treasure trove of subtle fashion. We suggest you visit Bibi's for a relaxed brunch, pop next door to buy a new hat or dress, then return to your table to sample the aforementioned sponges and bakes.

Sisters Maisha and Petria Lenehan have created an interesting focal point for the neighbourhood and they enjoy a loyal following. Word of warning: the proximity of the seats means this is not a good spot for letting slip some salacious gossip, unless you want to share it with the rest of the room.

● Mains: €6.40-€13.95
● Wine: BYOB

OPENING: Lunch: Mon-Fri
Brunch: Sat-Sun

**BOOKING:** No reservations

# BIJOU

46-47 Highfield Road,
Rathgar,
Dublin 6.

*www.bijourathgar.ie*

As winter approaches you'll not only appreciate Bijou for their hearty, comforting dishes (the glazed shank of lamb with creamed potato and root vegetables at €16.30 seems to be the talk of the town these days), but as of November 2011, you'll also be able to alleviate that cabin fever with a cosy meal on their new heated outdoor terrace. Still Bijou by name, no longer bijou by nature. Michelin star chef Errol Defoe and the rest of the team – who have the self-proclaimed curse of always being on the go (we think it's a blessing) – have extended their menu on both floors, meaning more choice for those of you who like to switch it up. We can't get enough of their signatures, like the confit duck leg with herb mash, braised red cabbage and duck jus for just €17.50. If you're looking for an early dinner, you'll want to avail of their early evening set menu for €19.95 (two courses). Or, if you like to dine out for your Sunday lunch, they offer a delicious set menu for the same price. Ice-cream with your banana crepe? Yeah, we could go there. Again and again.

- Starters: €5.75-€11.50
- Mains: €15.85-€29.95
- House Wine: €20

**OPENING:** Lunch: Mon-Sun
Dinner: Mon-Sun

**BOOKING:** Tel: 496 1518, reservations@bijourathgar.ie

# Santa Rita 120

## A TRADITION OF HONOURING HEROES

Chile, 1814. 120 brave men, led by Irishman Bernardo O'Higgins, take refuge from Chile's war of independence in the Santa Rita cellars. Our 120 range is named in their honour.

Today, Ireland's traditions and talent are brought to life by our musical heroes entertaining audiences around the world.

NOMINATE YOUR HERO TODAY AND WIN €10,000 FOR YOUR LOCAL COMMUNITY AND A TRIP TO CHILE.

120

HONOURING 120
PATRIOTS WHO
HELPED LEAD
CHILE TO
INDEPENDENCE

Cabernet
Sauvignon  VALLE CENTRAL CHILE

Santa Rita

**NOMINATE YOUR LOCAL HERO TODAY**

Find us on
Facebook

Enjoy SANTA RITA Sensibly
Visit drinkaware.ie

# BLOOM BRASSERIE

11 Upper Baggot Street,
Dublin 4.
www.bloombrasserie.ie

I f he ever decides to leave cooking behind him, owner/ chef of Bloom Brasserie Pól Ó hÉannraich could make a good living impersonating Roger Federer, as he is the born image of the swoony Swiss tennis star. We just thought you should know, lest you see Pól around the place and get afeared that Federer is rustling up your starter. But we're digressing. The stark, angular simplicity of the dining room is pleasingly unfussy and the clientele range from young professionals streaming in post-work from Baggot Street to the well-to-do seasoned diners from D4, who can sniff out a good restaurant at 60 paces. Both of these factors give the basement a somewhat cosmopolitan feel; you could just as easily be chowing down in a trendy NYC establishment. Like his doppelgänger Roger, Pól works non-stop with the restaurant serving (see what we did there?) lunch, dinner and even an extensive tapas menu, lest you're not quite hungry enough to tackle a full meal. We'd recommend trying their lemon, garlic and herb sautéed gambas (€7.95), which will make even the most refined diner want to lick their plate. Yep, in terms of champion grub, Bloom triumphs, game, set and match... Okay, we'll stop with the comparisons now.

- Starters: €6-15
- Mains: €16-27
- House Wine: €25

OPENING: Lunch: Mon-Fri
Dinner: Mon-Sat

**BOOKING:** Tel: 668 7170, email: info@bloombrasserie.ie

# BON APPETIT

9 James Terrace,
Malahide, Co. Dublin.
*www.bonappetit.ie*

**W**e've always loved Bon Appetit for their classy Georgian get-up, harbour view and their brasserie or fine dining restaurant options (depending on our mood), but when we heard they were opening a glamourous tapas bar, we had to check it out. Tapas seems to be the name of the game this year and 'Le Bon Vin', as the addition has been called, has already slipped seamlessly in with its longer-established peers. Perfect if you have a hankering for some late-week cocktails and calamari (or if you've forgotten to make a reservation at the restaurant or brasserie, as no reservations are required here). As always, if you do make it up to the restaurant on the first floor, you won't be disappointed – especially if you opt for the signature roast Norwegian halibut and Morteau sausage. Enjoy this along with your choice of starter and dessert (we always love the oxtail) with half a bottle of wine for €59.95. Or, if you're feeling slightly less indulgent, you can order off the three-course early bird menu for €29. For those of you looking to hone your own cooking skills, Bon Appetit offers masterclasses with head chef and restaurant owner Oliver Dunne. Includes refreshments and taster plates so you can reward yourself for your efforts.

- Starters: €6.50-11.50
- Mains: €16.50-31.50
- 3 course dinner €59.95
- 7 course dinner €69.95
- House Wine: €24

**OPENING:** Lunch: Wed-Sun
Dinner: Tues-Sat

**BOOKING:** Tel: 845 0314, email: reservations@bonappetit.ie

# LE BON CRUBEEN

81-82 Talbot Street,
Dublin 1.

*www.leboncrubeen.ie*

On a recent trip to the Abbey Theatre, that age-old question arose – where to eat that's within post-dinner dashing distance of the theatre, and, of course, enjoyable? Enter Le Bon Crubeen, the perfect location for such a bite. On that last visit we sauntered over there expecting to get a table with ease, but they were fully booked... on a Tuesday... at 6pm! Happily, they could seat us at the bar, which despite not being quite as comfortable as their proper tables is nonetheless perfectly functional for the speedy eater. The good news here is that they are currently extending the restaurant to add an extra 18 seats. Yes, the place is popular and rightly so. Their distinctive brand of no-nonsense good food at ridiculously reasonable prices proves that you can dine well for less these days without compromising on quality. Exciting news is that they've just hired a new head chef, Sam Byrne, whose CV boasts of a spell in the exclusive elBulli restaurant, where he was mentored by the legendary Ferran Adriài Acosta. As a result, they promise re-imagined menus that will hold to their ethos. We await this with bated breath and will be making sure to book in advance next time we visit.

- Starters: €4.95-7.50
- Mains: €10-12.50
- House Wine: €19

OPENING: Lunch: Mon-Sat
Dinner: Mon-Sun

**BOOKING:** Tel: 704 0126, email: info@leboncrubeen.ie

# THE BOX TREE

Stepaside Village,
Stepaside, Co. Dublin
www.theboxtree.ie

**NEW ENTRY**

Stepaside is one of those Dublin locations that people have heard of but can't quite place... a bit like Poppintree or Strawberry Beds. For the uninitiated, it is less than 10 minutes by car from Dundrum Town Centre. Even so, many still consider it to be a countrified locale, nestled as it is in the foothills of Three Rock Mountain. Ten years ago, the village boasted little more than a pub, a bookies and a pitch and putt course. Food options were just as limited. The Box Tree and the adjacent gastro pub The Wild Boar have upped the ante significantly. Prolific chef and restaurateur Eamonn O'Reilly of One Pico and Bleu Bistro Moderne heads up the operation and though the restaurant is only a year old, it already has an established feel (further proof being its recently earned Michelin Bib Gourmand). Expect classic, unpretentious dishes that showcase local produce with a nod to the village's rustic feel. Their vegetables are grown on their own farm in Kilternan, the dry-aged steaks are served on handcrafted slate trays and the desserts are nothing short of sublime. The *piece de resistance* is the hot chocolate fondant with crème Anglaise and orange chocolate ice-cream (€8.30), which may cause temporary blindness.

- Starters: €6.95-11.50
- Mains: €5.20-13.95
- House Wine: €19.90

OPENING: Lunch: Mon-Sun
Dinner: Mon-Sun

**BOOKING:** Tel: 205 2025

# BRASSERIE LE PONT

25 Fitzwilliam Place,
Dublin 2.
www.brasserielepont.ie

NEW ENTRY

A warm welcome to our list as one of Dublin's most stylish new restaurants. The vaguely pretentious name is derived from the location at the Leeson Street end of Fitzwilliam Street, near the bridge over the Grand Canal. We like the room, L-shaped and dressed up in warm-though-neutral shades. There's an imposing bar – it would be nice to sit there and just have a glass or two of wine if that's allowed – and an outdoor terrace. The chef is James Doyle, formerly of Ramsay at Powerscourt and the late, unlamented Gary Rhodes' D7, ably assisted by well-trained, smiley waiting staff. On our last visit we kicked off with a prawn cocktail, retro but currently enjoying a new vogue, consisting of large, soft-textured prawns, more like langoustine tails, contrasted nicely with crisp lettuce (€12.95). Our main course was a roast rack of Slaney Valley new season lamb (€23.95). We never considered just two cutlets a rack but this is offset by the inclusion of three small tasty rissoles made from shreds of shoulder and the whole dish was prettily garnished. Of the desserts, the tarte aux citron brulée with raspberry sorbet (€7.45) is a clear winner. Comfortable and classy, Brasserie Le Pont bridges the gap nicely between the formalised restaurant and the exuberant eatery.

- Starters: €4.95-14.50
- Mains: €12.95-29.95
- House Wine: €21

OPENING: B/fast & Lunch:
Mon-Fri  Dinner: Tues-Sat

**BOOKING:** Tel: 669 4600

# CAFÉ BAR H

Grand Canal Plaza,
Dublin 2.

www.cafebarh.ie

NEW ENTRY

Café Bar H is a collaboration between the amiable Rita Crosbie, wife of Harry, who, according to Rita "will be doing the washing up" and Johnny Cooke, that talented chef whose twice-demised eponymous restaurant was emblematic of the Jazz Age decadence of turn of the century Dublin. In Café Bar H, the interior decorator did their best to negate the impersonality of the large windows, and this surprisingly cosy room is redolent of similar establishments in Barcelona or San Sebastian. A curious nod to Dublin design heritage comes in the shape of imposing torch-bearing figures on the bar counter – they are an original fixture of the Shelbourne Hotel before its refurbishment. The young staff are welcoming, briskly efficient and seem to take pride in the food. We're delighted to report that the shared tapas bear no resemblance to the sad-looking 'snack on a saucer' that you'll find elsewhere. This is serious, fun food, perfectly cooked from righteous ingredients. The kind of meal you want to share with a big group of friends over a steady supply of Rioja. There is a lively atmosphere most nights. Expect to be gorging on generous portions of flavoursome creations involving squid, chorizo, Serrano ham and tomatoes, with the odd smear of truffle oil.

- Starters: €3-10
- Mains: €10-15
- House Wine: €24

OPENING: Lunch: Mon-Sat
Dinner: Mon-Sat

**BOOKING:** Tel: 899 2216

# THE CAKE CAFE

Daintree Building,
Pleasants Place, Dublin 8.
www.thecakecafe.ie

**W**e were surprised at how many people seemed unaware of this precious little gem, which admittedly can be missed as its main entrance is through the Daintree stationery store at Pleasants Place. An impossibly sequestered yet open location (you'll feel like you're on holiday with the pleasantly private and greenery-laden outdoor dining tables) means the party is happening outside (though the indoor seating area – albeit a small one – is nice as well). After ordering, you won't mind waiting for your food here as you can take the time to inspect their bizarre collection of dishes and cutlery that will have been laid out before you. We love coming here for breakfast, as their baked egg and bacon is unparalleled. Also a guaranteed warm-me-up for the winter months is their seasonally changing hot pot (exactly what it sounds like), a steaming mix of hearty and healthy goodness. If you like your cinnamon, vanilla and spice, a must-try beverage here is their chai tea latte, which is typically hard to find around these parts. Pair that with a slice of lemon cake (it is the Cake Cafe after all) and a glass of Prosecco, and you'll be walking on sunshine, no matter the weather.

- Mains: €4.95-8.90
- House Wine: €19

OPENING: Lunch: Mon-Sat
Dinner: Tues-Fri

**BOOKING:** No reservations

# CAMDEN KITCHEN

3a Camden Market,
Grantham Street, Dublin 8.
www.camdenkitchen.ie

**N**amed for its intimate atmosphere, Camden Kitchen will make you feel right at home with its small, cosy feel and ever-friendly staff. Since it opened in April, those frequenting the place have been lining up for their delicious French-style seasonal dishes and signature rabbit ballotine (a rabbit and pancetta ballotine with handmade potato gnocchi, black pudding and cauliflower puree, dubbed "a triumph" by our previous restaurant reviewer Ernie Whalley), but now there's even more reason to head to the Kitchen, especially for those brew connoisseurs among you. They now offer a variety of artisan draught beer on tap, both downstairs and in the function room bar upstairs. This is something we can really get behind – at least some of the city's restaurateurs are cottoning on to the fact

- Starters: €6.50-12
- Mains: €16-24
- House Wine: €22

OPENING: Lunch: Tues-Sat
Dinner: Tues-Sat

that we don't stick to the old reliables by preference and we actually love the burgeoning micro brewery output in the city. While you're at it, get a two-course early bird meal for €18 or a three-course meal for €23.50. Try their fillet of fresh fillet & chorizo casserole (€19.50), or for a light yet filling vegetarian option, the butternut squash ravioli with Cashel Blue, baby spinach and pumpkin seeds (€16.50). A perfect casual and homely dining experience.

**BOOKING:** Tel: 476 0125

# CANAL BANK CAFE

146 Upper Leeson Street,
Dublin 4.
www.tribeca.ie

**NEW ENTRY**

**W**e always kid ourselves that we won't order the spicy buffalo chicken wings (€12.95) before we arrive at Canal Bank Cafe, but resistance is futile. The second you walk in, that intoxicating vinegary deliciousness has you under its spell. What *do* they put in that sauce? And there are lots of other tasty offerings aside from the wings. The starter of crab with apple and fennel salad, tarragon cream dressing and proper homemade brown bread (€10.50) is a fresh start to the evening. And if you make it past the rookie error of ordering a whole basket of wings as a starter for yourself (trust us, always share), the fish and chips at €18.95 is yummy. We especially like the window seats as the smokers at O'Briens across the way always make for interesting people-watching, especially as an evening progresses and they become increasingly inebriated. Jim Sheridan likes this place too and was spotted having a fine old time the last time we went. All in all, Canal is a very nice solution to that pesky 'where do we go for a casual bite?' dilemma that often hits midweek, and can see one falling face first into a Big Mac meal if not careful.

- Starters: €5.95-12.95
- Mains: €10.95-24.95
- House Wine: €21

OPENING: Lunch: Mon-Sun
Dinner: Mon-Sun

**BOOKING:** Tel: 664 2135, email: info@tribeca.ie

# CAVISTONS

58-59 Glasthule Road,
Sandycove,
Co. Dublin
www.cavistons.com

It's almost a tradition in this guide for us to plead with restaurateur Peter Caviston to open for dinner more than two nights a week. We're asking him again to consider our plea as we think it's a crying shame that we can't pop out to Glasthule on a Wednesday evening to enjoy his famous hospitality. Begging done, we shall have to content ourselves with their lunches until he acquiesces. But let's face it, lunch at Cavistons is no consolation prize. There is simply nothing nicer than an afternoon spent sipping on a nice glass recommended by the knowledgeable staff while shucking an oyster or wrestling with a crevette. Don't let that *vino* go to your head though, because the menu tends to be a little pricey and if you don't keep an eye on your pennies things can easily spiral out of control. However, they do have an early bird menu from 6pm-6.30pm which is only €19.95 for two courses or €24.95 for three. Bargain! Menus change depending on what the fishermen haul in that day, but their current signature dish is scallops with roast red peppers, olive oil and garlic served with salad and potato (€24.50). Simple yet truly delicious.

- Starters: €5.95-10.95
- Mains: €10-25
- House Wine: €24

OPENING: Lunch: Tues-Sat
Dinner: Fri-Sat

**BOOKING:** Tel: 280 9245

# CHEZ MAX

133 Lower Baggot Street,
Dublin 2.
www.chezmax.ie

A restaurant so French we often expect to find Gerard Depardieu lurking somewhere on the premises, sucking on a Gauloise and necking Andie MacDowell (or wetting his pants). Anyway, their commitment to providing us with all things Gallic as part of the dining experience is admirable. From the chanteuse music wafting through the air, to the posters and random wine bottles dotted around the room, it's the little things like this that help to make a 45-minute lunch break feel like a quick trip to the Left Bank. Plus, having a glass of *vino* at lunch isn't frowned upon. While the original location on Castle Street is as enticing as ever, the Baggot Street branch of this Napoleonic empire is our favourite because of their wonderful terrace out back, which in the summer months is the perfect spot to catch some rays and spy on the talent. While they do serve frogs' legs and snails, (both €10.50) we'd recommend their boeuf bourguignon (€16.) If you're after a sandwich or cafe au lait on the go, the little coffee shop upstairs is handy too. They tell us Ryan Tubridy and Andrea Corr have been known to frequent, not together mind you – those kind of shenanigans would be too French.

- Starters: €5.90-16.50
- Mains: €9.50-24.50
- House Wine: €19

OPENING: Lunch: Mon-Sat
Dinner: Mon-Sun

**BOOKING:** Tel: 661 8899

# CHINA SICHUAN

Ballymoss Road, Sandyford
Industrial Estate, Dublin 18.
www.china-sichuan.ie

The Sichuan was something of a local treasure when it was based in Kilmacud. The family-run restaurant was ensconced there for 30 years and maintained a loyal client base thanks to the consistently good food and affable service. It has since moved to altogether more modern premises in Sandyford Industrial Estate, an area that, during the boom years, was tipped as The Next Big Thing. The current landscape of empty shells and broken dreams would tell a different story. Even so, the China Sichuan is always busy, no doubt because of the meticulous customer service... not to mention the glut of parking spaces and access to the Luas. It even offers a free taxi service on Saturday night (for journeys of no longer than five miles). As the name suggests, the restaurant specialises entirely in uniquely hot or 'tongue-numbing' dishes from the Sichuan region. While you'll need a jug of water on hand for some of them, remember that the recipes have been tempered slightly for Western palates. The hottest dish on the menu – in both senses of the word – is the spicy 3 pepper rib-eye beef: mature rib-eye seasoned with black pepper, five spice and sichuan pepper and panfried with dry chillies and pak choi (€21). Not for the faint-hearted.

- Starters: €5.50-12.50
- Mains: €12-35
- House Wine: €20

OPENING: Lunch: Mon-Fri &
Sun. Dinner: Mon-Sun

**BOOKING:** Tel: 293 5100, or book online

# CLIFF TOWN HOUSE

22 Saint Stephen's Green, Dublin 2.
www.theclifftownhouse.com

"**R**eally good seafood." This is what the Cliff Town House tell us they do best and we can vouch for that, such is the quality of their delicacies from the sea. While delicious in its simplicity, really awesome seafood (the kind they produce daily) requires great skill, which their head chef, Sean Smith, has in spades. Kudos to him. We are also happy to report that The Cliff Town House has shaken off the spectre of Bentley's, which used to occupy the building, and in the year and a bit since owner Barry O'Callaghan took over, has gained its own army of dedicated diners who just love the elegance and glamour that this top location possesses. If you've never been, there is a classy thrill inherent in ascending the grand Georgian steps to a restaurant on Stephen's Green. While it's a super spot for dates, engagements and impressing the in-laws, we'd particularly recommend a visit for anyone who is squeamish about the idea of eating oysters. There is no better place to face the fear than in the beautiful royal blue dining room. In fact, you'll feel like a right plum if you chicken out and don't give them a go (they start at €14.50 for six Galway specimens). Actor Sean Penn is a fan of this place.

- Starters: €8-18.00
- Mains: €17-35
- House Wine: €23

OPENING: Lunch: Mon-Sun
Dinner: Mon-Sun

**BOOKING:** Tel: 638 3939, or book online

# COPPINGER ROW

1 Coppinger Row, off South
William Street, Dublin 2.
www.coppingerrow.com

Head chef Ed Daly must have been nervous taking the reins at Coppinger Row last May. After all, he had big shoes to fill following the departure of the legendary Troy Maguire. But thankfully for diners, the transition between the two chefs has been seamless – we're not sure our stomachs could have coped with any kind of drop in standards. Potential crisis averted, owners Conor and Marc Bereen continue with their winning formula of precisely cooked but affordable Mediterranean dishes that utilise the finest ingredients this island has to offer. Case in point is the chargrilled rib-eye with horseradish, celeriac and watercress salad served with roasted bone marrow (€26). Yes it is as delicious as it sounds. First-time visitors are advised to try the set evening menu which is €25 for two courses and €30 for three, as it offers an exciting and affordable introduction to the kind of food they serve. Anyone who has wandered in and staggered out will also wax lyrical about the appeal of their cocktails and alcoholic coffees, not to mention the general buzz – this place is always busy with a cosmopolitan crowd. They also serve all through the afternoon, so if you end up lunching a bit later than most you won't miss out on their top-notch nosh.

- Starters: €6-13.50
- Mains: €13.50-19.50
- House Wine: €20

OPENING: Lunch: Mon-Sun
Dinner: Mon-Sun

**BOOKING:** Tel: 672 9884, email: info@coppingerrow.com (Parties of 6+)

# DAKSHIN

22-24 Donnybrook,
Dublin 4.

www.dakshin.ie

NEW ENTRY

**D**akshin is an ancient Sanskrit word for 'south'. The owner Saji Mathai is from Southern India, as is the cuisine, a mix of classic dishes from the states of Kerala, Tamilnadu, Andhra Pradesh and Karnataka. The restaurant is a new addition to the Donnybrook culinary landscape, occupying a space over Kielys pub. The restaurant has since been extensively refurbished to create a bright, modern dining room with the occasional Eastern flourish. Dakshin was always going to deliver. Saji and his team have all served their time with the Jaipur group, which pioneered upmarket Indian cuisine in Dublin. While they specialise in location-specific dishes such as traditional Keralan lamb stew (€17.50) and Alleppey prawn curry – griddled jumbo prawns cooked with raw mango, green chilli, ginger and coconut milk (€18.50) – they also serve up hall of famers like chicken tikka masala and lamb rogan josh with brio. Vegetarians will appreciate the perfectly cooked dal (lentils), dosa (rice and lentil pancakes with cheese, coriander, onion and tomato) and the excellent selection of naan breads. A well-considered and decently-priced wine list and cocktail menu completes the offering. Check out the value menu: €18 for two courses, all day Sun-Wed, and Thurs-Sat until 7pm.

- Starters: €6.50-12.50
- Mains: €15.50-22
- House Wine: €18

OPENING: Dinner: Mon-Sun

**BOOKING:** Tel: 202 8182, email: info@dakshin.ie

# DIEP LE SHAKER

55 Pembroke Lane,
Dublin 2.
www.diep.net

There has been an injection of youthful thinking at Diep Le Shaker since owner Mathew Farrell brought his children Matt and Alex on board. They're responsible for the quirky Bangkok Street Lunch menu, which includes soup, appetiser and main course (€10.95) and the live music nights during which they host local blues and funk band Mob Fandango, and Richard Farrell of erstwhile band, History of Harry (who, incidentally, is yet another Farrell scion). Even though the younger members of the Farrell clan are all about capturing the Zeitgeist, the initial inception of the Diep empire on Pembroke Lane is still stuck back in 1999, meaning they are still serving some of the best Thai food in Dublin. The chefs fly all their ingredients in from Bangkok and their endeavours for authenticity have been noted by the prestigious Thailand Brand Award awarded by the Government of Thailand. Try the Chiang Mai pork lollipops (€7.50) and the classic Pad Thai (€14.50). Those watching their funds can plump for the value menu: the three-course meal for two and a bottle of wine for €60, available Tuesday-Friday. Failing that, you could get a Diep Home, another brainchild of the younger Farrells.

- Starters: €7-10.50
- Mains: €12.50-29.50
- House Wine: €20

OPENING: Lunch: Tues-Fri
Dinner: Tues-Sat

**BOOKING:** Tel: 661 1829, email: reservations@diep.net

# THE DYLAN

Dylan Hotel, Eastmoreland
Place, Dublin 4
www.dylan.ie

NEW ENTRY

Walking into this ever-so chic hotel, restaurant and bar still feels like stepping into a feature in *Wallpaper* magazine. Inside this unassuming, classically beautiful Victorian building, you find an explosion of modern baroque splendour, like the contents of a particularly decadent interior designer's mind had been emptied out into the corridors. We love the *Alice-in-Wonderland*-esque oversized chairs and gaudy mirror frames. The Hong Kong edition of *Time Out* magazine impressed too. In the summer, the outside terrace for the restaurant is one of the most idyllic spots to lounge in the city. The dining room itself is smart yet intimate. Chef Richard Carmody's strong, indulgent, traditionally Irish cooking was a big hit at last year's Taste of Dublin festival. For dinner, order the magnificent seared king scallops with crispy slow-roasted pork belly, prepared with cherry tomato, basil pesto and balsamic reduction (€12.50). Follow with spring lamb chops, creamy gratin potatoes, tomatoes and grilled courgette (€26.95). If you are feeling particularly affluent then the whole 'Lobster Lawyer' in a creamy white wine sauce and tomato concasse finished with whiskey (€35) is, quite frankly, sensational.

- Starters: €8.50-12.50
- Mains: €18-35
- House Wine: €24.50

OPENING: Lunch: Tues-Sun
Dinner: Tues-Sun

BOOKING: Tel: 660 3000, email: justask@dylan.ie

# ELY

22 Ely Place,
Dublin 2.

www.elywinebar.ie

**T**he Dubliner HQ is a prime location for easy access to Erik and Michelle Robson's Ely Wine Bar (going over a decade strong), and since our very first visit we've thoroughly enjoyed this place, whether it be for lunch, dinner or a more liquid-fuelled affair. This elegant spot, though often bustling, possesses the mystical ability to somehow seem quiet mid-week, which makes it a great place to clear your mind and slip away from busy surrounds (or have a sneaky lunch-time date). When we went for lunch recently, we had the sandwich of the day (an expertly seasoned chicken sandwich – harder to master than you'd think) with hand-cut chips, for only €9.75. It wasn't a hair short of phenomenal. Our starter salads of tomato, basil, mozzarella, cucumber and mint with a sherry vinaigrette also didn't disappoint, as they were fresh and crisp (another thing which shouldn't be difficult to execute, but we've certainly had our fair share of soggy and older-than-they-should-be salads). Their signature is the organic Burren beef burger (€15.50) and we understand why; Knockanore smoked Irish cheddar and chilli sauce serve as the juiciest possible cherry on top of this beefcake. And don't forget the wines – they have 500 bins.

- Starters: €6.25-14.50
- Mains: €14.50-28.95
- House Wine: €24

OPENING: Lunch: Mon-Sat
Dinner: Mon-Sat

**BOOKING:** Tel: 676 8986, email: elyplace@elywinebar.com

# FALLON & BYRNE

17 Exchequer Street,
Dublin 2.
www.fallonandbyrne.com

**NEW ENTRY**

Every time we walk past Fallon & Byrne that photograph of Bill Clinton on the wall by the front door never fails to catch our eye. For those who haven't seen it, the snap shows the former US President visiting the establishment. Mind you, we really didn't need his endorsement to decide how fabulous this place is. From the naughty delights of the basement wine bar, to the wholesome groceries and deli counter delights on the ground floor, and the delicious offerings of the first floor restaurant, this place is a foodie's delight. Here, it's the first floor restaurant that we're going to give most of our attention to. Under the helm of head chef Tom Meenaghan, they dish up the kind of food that lodges in your memory, and means you will wake up in the middle of the night craving a meal there. Their beef is especially tasty. All of it is aged for at least 21 days, and you can really taste this. You can really notice this quality when sampling their signature dish of aged Irish fillet of beef, panacalty potato, confit shallot and port reduction (€30.75); truly a carnivore's wet dream.

- Starters: €5.70-13.50
- Mains: €17.30-30.75
- House Wine: €22

**OPENING:** Lunch: Mon-Sat
Dinner: Mon-Sat

**BOOKING:** Tel: 472 1000, email: restaurant@fallonandbyrne.com

# FIRST FLOOR @ HARVEY NICHOLS

Dundrum Town Centre,
Sandyford Road, Dublin 16.
www.harveynichols.com

The first thing to mention is this is a fun restaurant. You *will* order dessert and you *will* have that extra glass of wine, so don't feel guilty about it. The dining room has been designed to make you feel at ease with indulgence. In fact, feel free to move next door to the phenomenal cocktail bar after your meal and order a cosmopolitan. Before that, gasp at the tasty morsels designed by Chef de Cuisine Philip Mahon (formerly of Mint and Gordon Ramsay at Powerscourt). The thing to order here is the pan-fried seabass (€24.50). The most delectable fillet is prepared with a gorgeous medley of borlotti bean, chorizo, courgette and olive. The menu changes regularly to keep things interesting. "Cooked with thought" is their motto and this mantra certainly shows on the plate. David

- Starters: €7.50-11.50
- Mains: €18.50-24.50
- House Wine: €18.50

OPENING: Lunch: Tues-Sun
Dinner: Tues-Sat

O'Brien is the manager, and his staff have been well-trained to make sure you feel welcome and relaxed here. The set price lunch menu of two courses for €18.50 is great value. The dining room has seen some changes recently, the crisp white table cloths disappearing in favour of attractive wooden table tops. Sometimes restaurants that open in a purpose-built new space take a while to get comfortable and we get the sense that this place is just getting into its stride.

**BOOKING:** Tel: 291 0488, email: firstfloor.reservations@harveynichols.

# FOODGAME

## 10 South Lotts Road, Dublin 4

www.facebook.com/foodgame

NEW ENTRY

**T**he latest arrival on the Beggar's Bush culinary block (the crossroads between Bath Avenue, Grand Canal Street, South Lott's Road and Shelbourne Road) is this breakfast/lunch/deli spot down the side of South Lott's Road opposite Slattery's pub. This area used to be a gastronomic desert, counting three pubs and one greasy spoon. Now we have Juniors, Paulie's Pizza, the Chop House and this new kid. The vibe on this corner demands good buzz, good value and keeping things simple. (Well, the Chop House prices itself up a bit). Foodgame does all that. It's all clean lines and cosiness – an upmarket deli with pasta, cakes and delicious jars of things for sale, a big table, a few counters and an open-plan kitchen (well, hot plates). In keeping with the New York vibe, chef-proprietor Ross Staunton arrives on his bike. He's Ballymaloe-trained so knows how to make simple things work, and work well. For lunch try the soup and sandwich combo (€6/€5 take away) – that's delicious home-made soup like carrot and coriander and solid sandwiches of brie or chicken. Breakfast is creamy scrambled eggs with chives (€6), or muesli with yoghurt. And the coffee is among the best in Dublin.

- Starters: €3-7
- Mains: €3-7
- House Wine: €16.50

OPENING: Mon-Fri: 8am-6pm.
Sat-Sun: 9.30am-3.30pm

**BOOKING:** Tel: 281 5002, email: foodgamedublin@gmail.com

# GOOD WORLD

18 South Great George's Street, Dublin 2.

**NEW ENTRY**

There are a multitude of Chinese restaurants in Dublin these days. Lots have sprung up on Parnell Street, which has become a mecca for those in search of the sweet, sour and spicy. However, the young contenders can't hold a candle to the long-established brilliance of Good World on George's Street. Proprietors Yuen Fun Tsang and Hon Ki Lau bring 20 years of experience to the table, producing all your favourite dishes as well as a few more unusual offerings if you're feeling brave – there are two menus, one in English and one in Chinese (which those in the know order from). That being said it is their dim-sum that most people leave raving about, and one visit here will leave you craving more. Ranging in price from €3.60-€4.50, these little parcels of delight are expertly steamed so as never to be soggy, rather light and unbelievably moreish. You can find yourself going all Cookie Monster on them, devouring one after another. Incidentally, the staff are that brilliant mix of attentive yet discreet, covertly keeping an eye on you to make sure you're not wanting for water or left with plates on the table for too long, which is an underrated skill in our book.

- Starters: €3.60-14.80
- Mains: €12-18.60
- House Wine: €18

OPENING: Lunch: Mon-Sun
Dinner: Mon-Sun

**BOOKING:** Tel: 677 5373

# THE GREEN HEN

33 Exchequer Street,
Dublin 2.
*www.thegreenhen.com*

This colourful, art-laden spot is a feast for the eyes and for the mouth. Whether you come here for a drink (some have dubbed the Green Hen's 'Old Fashioned' cocktail, €9.50, the best in the country – quite a compliment) at their convivial Zinc bar, where slick-looking twenty-somethings make eyes at each other all weekend long, or a bite (their duck confit, €19, left one reader's "mouth watering for days afterward" – not sure if that's really such a compliment), you're bound to leave either happy or hooked-up. A special perk as well (provided you are not some bizarrely cultured and well-read child that has, for whatever reason, pinched this guide off your dad) means guaranteed peaceful dining after 5pm, as kids under 12 will not be admitted after this time. We like the (no) sound of that. It might be a hindrance to some, but you know you'll be grateful when you find yourself time travelling back to your carefree childless days like those of the early twenty-somethings at the bar... unless you got started young and have long forgotten the taste of sweet freedom. Bottoms up? PS, try to bag a table upstairs. It feels like dining in someone's particularly swish living room.

- Starters: €6-10
- Mains: €15-24
- House Wine: €22

OPENING: Lunch: Mon-Fri
Dinner: Mon-Sun

**BOOKING:** Tel: 670 7238

# GREEN NINETEEN

19 Camden Street Lower,
Dublin 2.

www.green19.ie

**S**o a couple of the mains have sneaked above the €10 mark (the duck cassoulet and the braised beef bourguignon are both €13.50), but Green Nineteen is still one of the best value eateries on the block. Pioneers of low-cost but high-quality dining, brothers Colin and Adam Dixon seem to know exactly what people want these days. Their comfort food has struck a chord with Dubliners in the three years since this restaurant has been open, ensuring its enduring popularity. It also helps that the restaurant is located on the axis of hip that is Camden Street, and everyone knows hipsters don't cook for themselves. But we digress. We haven't even mentioned the drinks they offer yet and that's a very important part of this place's charm. For €9, they serve up some of the most keenly priced cocktails in the city. We're suckers for the Earl Grey gimlet, that's Earl Grey-infused gin, lime and sugar. Ah, mother's little helper! So what should you not miss if you go there? Well, we recommend trying to get in for brunch if you can, their grill 19 fry-up (€10) is a treat that is guaranteed to cure even the most nuclear of hangovers.

- Starters: €4-8
- Mains: €10-14
- House Wine: €16

OPENING: Lunch: Mon-Sun
Dinner: Mon-Sun

**BOOKING:** (dinner only) Tel: 478 9626, email: management@green19.ie

# HARTLEY'S

1 Harbour Road,
Dun Laoghaire,
Co. Dublin.
www.hartleys.ie

**NEW ENTRY**

**O**prah has coined the phrase 'live your best life' (and its acronym, LYBL, too). Though undeniable cheesy, it does spring to mind while at Hartley's during a certain sun-kissed time of day, sitting at one of their terraced tables (if it's warm enough), with one of their delicious mojitos in hand. Hartley's is the perfect seaside dining spot. Inside, the high ceilings and long tables make for an unusual dining room, but also provide a good balance for families, couples or a rowdy hungover table of many. Staff usually greet with a big, warm smile, and we like that. No matter what anyone says, that kind of thing makes you feel a little bit better than you did pre-smile. Delicious cocktails are matched by an equally impressive wine list, but of course, the food is what we're really there for. Specials can be hit and miss, so if you're playing it safe, go with what they're best at – seafood. The mussels to start at €9 are an undeniable winner and the beer battered halibut and chips (€25) comes with an addictive caper aioli (please sir, we want some more). Even if you don't LYBL, you'll at least *feel* like you are. Live it up at Hartley's.

- Starters: €8-13.50
- Mains: €14.50-28
- House Wine: €22

OPENING: Lunch: Tues-Sun
Dinner: Tues-Sun

**BOOKING:** Tel: 280 6767, email: info@hartleys.ie

# HONEST TO GOODNESS

25 Market Arcade,
George's Street, Dublin 2.
www.honesttogoodness.ie

**S**andwich making is an art and Dublin's old masters are Honest To Goodness. While other smaller emporiums have been forced to shut up shop, Darragh Birkett and Martin Ansbro just keep on trucking with their artisan daily offerings still luring us to the George's Street Arcade even six years after their opening. The devil is in the detail as they say, and it's the fact that they bake their own bread, make their own relishes and even roast their own meats that gives them an edge over their competitors. It wouldn't be *The Dubliner 100 Best Restaurants* if we didn't give a nod to our enduring love story: the Friday special. That is the sloppy joe (€6.95) a sandwich of spicy beef mince which remains our favourite thing on the menu (just don't try and eat two in one sitting, we learned that the hard way...). In the past two editions of this book, Honest to Goodness have mentioned that that they might be extending, but since these plans have yet to come to fruition, they won't be drawn on whether or not they'll be trying to extend this year, saying only, "we would like to break the trend and say nothing." Fingers crossed this is the year they take the plunge.

- Sandwiches: €5-6.95
- Salads: €6-7.95

OPENING: Lunch: Mon-Sun
Dinner: Mon-Sun

**BOOKING:** To pre-order, call 633 7727

# HUGO'S

6 Merrion Row,
Dublin 2.

www.hugos.ie

There is something terribly nice about going to Hugo's for lunch. Perhaps it's the dim lighting, the mixed-bag clientele or the feeling that you won't be judged for having a little tipple during the day, but as soon as you walk through the doors you instantly relax. The price of the set lunch is also a factor, as it remains one of the best bargains on Baggot Street with two courses a very affordable €15.50 and three just €20. Evenings are a slightly different kettle of fish. They maintain the same relaxed atmosphere, but it feels like chef Didier Rhodes has been let off the leash a little and his food really comes into its own when you have the time to linger over it. Try his signature dish, the free-range chicken breast filled with goats' cheese and wrapped in Serrano ham, served with pot barley risotto, grilled asparagus and a tarragon jus (€21). They have a pre-theatre menu which is €70 for two and they reckon *à la carte* works out at about €98, which in these tight times is reasonable for the excellent food on offer. Try and head there on a Thursday evening or for Sunday brunch when the food is accompanied by some live jazz.

- Starters: €6.80-8.75
- Mains: €18-27
- House Wine: €22.25

OPENING: Lunch: Mon-Sun
Dinner: Mon-Sun

**BOOKING:** Tel: 676 5955

# INDEPENDENT PIZZA CO.

28 Lower Drumcondra Road, Dublin 9.

NEW ENTRY

**O**n match days at Croke Park, some supporters choose to rely on a rake of pints alone for sustenance, while others are content to supplement their intake of stout by periodically picking their way through packets of Tayto. The clever ones know that they'll find the best local food at the bridge in Drumcondra. The small but perfectly formed Independent Pizza Company serve up some of the most innovative pizzas in the city. This will come as no surprise to those who have visited their sister venue, The Gotham Café on St Anne Street, over the last 20 years. On our last visit, we noticed the culchies in the room wasted their time with chicken caesar salad or lasagne. That's pleasant enough, inoffensive grub, but it's nothing compared to the tasty things this place does with a pizza base and Thai prawns, Spanish chorizo, barbeque duck, chillies or guacamole. Next time you're there, make sure to ask for our favourite, the Texas Chicken Pizza (€9.50), an 11-inch pizza crowned with a spicy tomato sauce, honey marinated chicken, roasted red onion, green pepper, mozzarella and asiago cheese with crème fraiche. Now that's a winner – and a much more satisfying post-match celebration than a visit to Copper Face Jacks.

- Starters: €2.65-6
- Mains: €6-13.75
- House Wine: €16.50

OPENING: Lunch: Mon-Sun
Dinner: Mon-Sun

**BOOKING:** 830 2044

# *Santa Rita* 120

## A TRADITION OF HONOURING HEROES

Chile. 1814. 120 brave men, led by Irishman Bernardo O'Higgins, take refuge from Chile's war of independence in the Santa Rita cellars. Our 120 range is named in their honour.

Ireland's literary heroes, both past and present, are renowned around the world for groundbreaking stories.

NOMINATE YOUR HERO TODAY AND WIN €10,000 FOR YOUR LOCAL COMMUNITY AND A TRIP TO CHILE.

120

HONOURING 120
PATRIOTS WHO
HELPED LEAD
CHILE TO
INDEPENDENCE

Chardonnay

D. O. VALLE CENTRAL CHILE

*Santa Rita*

Enjoy SANTA RITA Sensibly
Visit drinkaware.ie

**NOMINATE YOUR LOCAL HERO TODAY**

Find us on
Facebook

# ITSA4

6a Sandymount Green,
Dublin 4.

www.itsa.ie

NEW ENTRY

The chances are you have eaten something connected to Peaches and Domini Kemp's culinary network over the past 10 years. Perhaps an orange and almond cake (€3) in their café at IMMA or a healthy super food salad (€13.30) at The Restaurant in Brown Thomas. If you haven't picked up a chewy circle of deliciousness in one of their branches of Itsa bagel, then you should remedy this promptly. The two sisters have enjoyed tremendous success in a variety of guises. We're particularly enthusiastic about their slick, family-friendly restaurant on the green in Sandymount Village. Their menu is built around seasonal ingredients from a small but talented cadre of Irish artisan suppliers who provide the basis for head chef Paul Kavanagh's creations. If you're ever heading to a sporting event or concert nearby, it is worth remembering that you can order two courses for €20 any time on Tuesday to Friday or 6-7pm on Fridays and Saturdays. Try a starter of Moroccan chickpea and cumin salad, with feta cheese, lemon and chili oil, followed by salmon fillet and roast fennel, olives, grilled red onion, tomato and basil reduction. A much more appetising prelude to a Leinster match than a batter burger outside the stadium.

- Bagels: €5.90-10.95
- Mains: €15.50-21
- House Wine: €23

OPENING: Lunch: Tues-Sun
Dinner: Tues-Sun

**BOOKING:** 219 4676

# JAIPUR

41 George's Street,
Dublin 2

www.jaipur.ie

**R**eal Indian food arrived in this country when Jaipur first opened its doors in 1998. Before that, Indian food was bland and beige. This unassuming restaurant was the spark that ignited a passion for fiery flavours and a whole new palate of exotic tastes. The man behind it all is Asheesh Dewan who also has branches of Jaipur in Dalkey and Malahide. He seemed to enjoy the skepticism when he chose to open in unfashionable Ongar, now a successful and established suburban outpost. The menu varies slightly between each restaurant, often influenced by which region of India the chefs hail from. Our favourite remains the well-appointed yet casual city centre location. One of the most popular dishes is purdah gosht dumdaar (€21.95)– slow braised lamb cooked overnight on hot coals with aromatic spices served with roast potatoes and shallots and presented in a sealed pot. Many readers tell us that this is the best restaurant in the city for vegetarians; look out for the panchratan kofte (€15.50), five seasonal vegetable dumplings with nuts, cottage cheese and raisin in a creamy awadhi tomato sauce. Still capable of serving up a memorable meal, Jaipur is one of the few restaurants to feature in every edition of this book over the last decade.

- Starters: €6.95-14
- Mains: €19.95-25
- House Wine: €20

OPENING: Dinner: Mon-Sat

**BOOKING:** Tel: 677 0999, or book online

# JOHNNIE FOX'S

Glencullen,
Co. Dublin
www.jfp.ie

**C**ity folk invariably smirk at the trail of tourists heading up into the Dublin Mountains for Guinness and a plate of oysters, and no doubt a good helping of diddly-eye begorrah and begosh in a pub that feels like the set of a clichéd movie adapted from a Cecilia Ahern novel. Yet there is a great deal of post-ironic fun to be had here by even the most cynical. Portions are huge, prices have been reduced and the food is consistently good. Granted, the nightly show would not be to everyone's taste, but it provides raucous entertainment in an endearing, rambling old building. The Johnnie Fox's Hooley Experience (€48) is a four-course meal that includes live music and Irish dancing till midnight. Everyone should try it once. Seriously. At its heart this is a destination pub for more sedate evenings of conversation over a plate of steamed West Coast mussels in garlic and white wine sauce (€8.60) or slices of oak smoked salmon on brown bread (€7.20). Johnnie Fox's has been here for over 200 years; this doesn't seem to have held them back. Colin Farrell and American singer Pink are among those spotted recently enjoying dinner in front of the peat fire.

- Starters: €4.75-18.75
- Mains: €9.95-28.75
- House Wine: €21.90

OPENING: Lunch: Mon-Sun
Dinner: Mon-Sun

**BOOKING:** Tel: 295 5647

# JUNOS

26 Parkgate Street,
Dublin 8.
www.junoscafe.com

**J**unos is a bit of a
superhero restaurant.
A mild-mannered café
beloved of locals by day, like
Clark Kent taking off his
glasses, it transforms into a
bustling bistro that attracts hordes of foodies from across the city by
night. Opened in 2009, the restaurant has steadily gained devotees
with word-of-mouth playing a large part in their success; this place
has plenty of regulars. Finnish head chef Juha Salo's traditional-
style food, made using all Irish ingredients, shows the kind of flair
that only very accomplished chefs possess, so while dishes might
seem deceptively simple, serious skill is evident in each mouthful.
Case in point is his signature dish of leek and wild mushroom risotto
cake topped with Ryefield goats' cheese and a tomato and courgette
ragu (€14.50), which skillfully melds
together a multitude of flavours and
textures to produce something you will
later find yourself daydreaming about.
And don't even get us started on the
desserts here, which are as gigantic as
they are delicious. They have an early
bird menu from Tuesday until Saturday
(two courses €18.50, three courses
€23.50), but are devils for running offers
on the *à la carte* menu too, so keep a keen
eye out for those.

- Starters: €8.30-8.50
- Mains: €13.50-19
- House Wine: €19

**OPENING:** Lunch: Tues-Sat
Dinner: Mon-Sat

**BOOKING:** Tel: 670 9820, email: junoscafe@gmail.com

# KC PEACHES

28-29 Nassau Street,
Dublin 2.
www.kcpeaches.com

**NEW ENTRY**

Fans of the original KC Peaches on Pearse Street (which has been there for five years now) must have thought all their dreams had come true when a second restaurant opened on Nassau Street. Inches closer to the centre of town, this bright, airy premises is a welcome addition to an area which – bar a few hot food counters where Trinners students can buy breakfast rolls and spicy wedges – is sadly lacking in quality breakfast and lunch emporiums. The large windows, which let you gawk in and see what others are eating (and drool while you do so), also make it the perfect spot to do a bit of people-watching on a wet afternoon. But what about the food? Well, KC's boasts good, filling, healthy homemade fare, so salads, sarnie and soups abound. The discerning diner will probably like to know that they use no additives in their food, rely on local producers when they can and change the menus regularly so you won't get bored. Mind you, it's not all sensible. Their famous cakes are here too. Rather large, portions are best shared with friends, but be wary of a feeding frenzy ensuing. The fudge and walnut brownie (€3.50) is to die for.

- Cakes: €1.45-4
- Mains: €4.14-9.45
- House Wine: €15

OPENING: B/fast & Lunch:
Mon-Sun. Dinner: Mon-Fri

**BOOKING:** 633 5872

# KIMCHI

160 Parnell Street,
Dublin 1.
www.hophouse.ie

"**W**e're sure you can enjoy amazing time having brilliant foods with welcoming air, friendly staffs," reads the website for Kimchi. While this automatically disqualifies them from 'The Dubliner's 100 Most Grammatically Correct Restaurants', it at least gives the venue a certain charm. Kimchi is a form of Korean vegetable pickling that lends a piquant flavour to the food. Here it is mostly in the form of spicy fermented cabbage, which tastes infinitely better than it sounds. The most popular dishes are Bibimbap (€8.90): stirfried vegetables, minced beef or tofu, topped with egg yolk on a bed of rice in a stone bowl and Bulgogi: thin slices of marinated beef served on a sizzling pan with three side dishes. They've also recently added a decent sushi and sashimi menu. Kimchi is located in what was the Shakespeare Pub on Parnell Street (now the Hop House) but this isn't pub grub as we know it. There's no slapdash carveries or desserts festering under lights, like gamey auld ones in Coppers. However, should you be in the mood for a pint, they offer some tasty deals on pitchers. Expect a crowd of locals, trendies and thespians from the nearby Gate and Abbey theatres.

- Starters: €3.50-9.80
- Mains: €6.90-32
- House Wine: €18.90

**OPENING:** Lunch: Mon-Sun
Dinner: Mon-Sun

**BOOKING:** Tel: 872 8318

# KINGFISHER

166 Parnell Street,
Dublin 1.
www.kingfisherdublin.com

Tourists visiting the city should do themselves a favour and eschew the Oirish restaurant offerings of Temple Bar and instead, if they want to see a traditional Dublin restaurant, visit The Kingfisher. This family-owned Northside eatery has been trading for 40 years and once you've visited, prepare to be utterly smitten as the bantering staff give you a proper, BS-free céad mile failte alongside your feed. They consider the mixed grill (€14.95) a signature dish, but if you fancy this, go hungry and wear elasticated trousers because for that price you get a pork chop, two sausages, liver, bacon, egg, fried onion, chips, grilled tomato, peas or beans, a tea or coffee and a complimentary jelly and ice-cream. Desperately hungover? We would, quite literally, sell our grandmother for one of their all-day full Irish breakfasts (€9.95), which are impeccably executed (in all seriousness, it's very tough to get a fry right) and we believe they may have actual healing properties, like echinacea or whatever. All this, and we haven't even mentioned the cult-like following the fish and chips have. What do the Kingfisher think the reason is for their enduring popularity? "Nothing fancy, just good food, good prices and good service." Sounds about right.

- Starters: €3.50-6.95
- Mains: €5.50-19.95
- House Wine: €13.95

OPENING: Lunch: Mon-Sun
Dinner: Mon-Sun

**BOOKING:** 8728732, email: info@kingfisherdublin.com

# EVERY THURSDAY IN THE **Herald**

*www.facebook.com/thedublinermagazine*

# THE KING SITRIC

East Pier, Howth,
Co. Dublin
www.kingsitric.ie

**W**hat brought A-list stars in the order of Micheal Caine, Shirley Bassey, Sandra Bullock, Bruce Springsteen and Bon Jovi to the picturesque seaside village of Howth? The King Sitric, which has stood proudly on Howth's harbourside for almost 40 years. The owners abide by the 'if it's not broke...' adage. This is an old-school establishment for an old-school crowd. The focus is on fresh fish, which are caught just 400 metres from the front door. If you want to push your own boat out, plump for the unashamedly indulgent Lobster Share (€115 for two people). It includes three lobsters: one grilled, one steamed and one finished in a 'Dublin Lawyer Sauce'. For the uninitiated, the latter lobster is finished in a cream sauce, Irish whiskey, mustard and lemon juice. Why the name? "Some say the lawyers were the only ones who could afford the lobster." according to owners Aidan and Joan McManus. Patrons can also check into one of their eight sea-view rooms after dinner. All the bedrooms, named after lighthouses, are located overlooking Balscadden Bay. For more accessible prices, try the food in the recently opened Hugel Wine Bar, located, quite invitingly, in their wine cellar.

- 2 course dinner: €28
- 3 course dinner: €35
- House Wine: €24

**OPENING:** Lunch: Sunday
Dinner: Mon & Wed-Sat

**BOOKING:** Tel: 832 5225, email: info@kingsitric.ie

# L'ECRIVAIN

109a Lower Baggot St,
Dublin 2.

www.lecrivain.com

Though L'Ecrivain is something of a celebrity haunt, their ethos is totally egalitarian. They roll the red carpet out for all patrons to the degree that you're almost left wondering where exactly your limo is at going-home time. The Michelin-star establishment is by no means cheap, but the superlative service reminds you that you're here for an all-encompassing dining experience rather than a quick bite. Celebrated chef Derry Clarke, voted Santa Rita Chef's Chef 2012, mans the kitchen while his charming wife Sallyanne looks after the front of house, along with a team of expert waiting staff and sommeliers. It's all about the little touches here, from the freshly baked breads and amuse-bouches to the sing-songs around the grand piano. The Clarkes aren't only ambassadors for Irish cuisine – witnessed by the incredible array of homegrown produce on their menu – but ambassadors for Irishness, so warm is their welcome. Their lunch menu - €23.50 for three courses - is the ideal opportunity for those on a budget, but be warned, the hospitality here is so good that you may want to stay on and explore the extensive wine list... and the supplements on the menu may unwittingly push you into the red.

- 2 course dinner: €60
- 3 course dinner: €75
- House Wine: €23.50

OPENING: Lunch: Thurs-Fri
Dinner: Mon-Sat

**BOOKING:** Tel: 661.1919, www.lecrivain.com

# L'GUEULETON

1 Fade Street,
Dublin 2.
www.lgueuleton.com

**A**part from a few shuffles in the kitchen line-up, not much has changed at this place in the seven years since it opened. The dining room has the rustic charm it always had, the staff maintain their business-like demeanour and the diners are still a mixed bunch. But you know what they say, if it ain't broke... Their classic Gallic menu hasn't transformed much either, thankfully. A stalwart we're always glad to see is the French onion soup, a steaming bowl, chock full of onions and made naughty with a lump of gruyere melting into the top of it (€7.80). In the summer months (or if it's winter and you're a hardy person) make for the outside terrace which is one of the cutest in the city. We always forget that portions tend toward the massive, which should be kept in mind when ordering. They're currently setting up a new L'Gueuleton bar next door to the restaurant, which they tell us will be opening very soon. Considering the fact that they still don't do bookings, this will mean that deciding where to go if there's a wait for a table (it used to be a toss-up between the Long Hall and the Market Bar) will be a no-brainer.

- Starters: €3.50-12.50
- Mains: €14.50-26.50
- House Wine: €21.80

OPENING: Lunch: Mon-Sun
Dinner: Mon-Sun

**BOOKING:** No reservations

# L. MULLIGAN

18 Stoneybatter,
Dublin 7.

www.lmulligangrocer.com

When we first discovered this special spot about a year ago, it was early days and the focus was on their uniquely varied selection of speciality beers (no Heino here, thankfully). But hard to ignore was the unfinished vibe to the place, revolving around a mysterious Wizard of Oz-style curtain in the back of the room that signified no entry. As much as this stimulated the curiosity in us, we were happy to see it go, for its removal gave way to some additions of equally wizard-like magic: a fully extended space complete with a beer and herb garden, new taps, hand-hewn furniture and the like. That said, the beer garden can be a little distracting for conversation when the extractor fan is extracting such delicious smells from the kitchen.

Though the drinks are still a massive draw, L. Mulligan's expansion involves a fully fledged *à la carte* menu with weekly changing items matched with a whiskey and beer. Some gems on the menu are the scotch egg with leek and cheddar, and the freshly made black pudding with rhubarb relish and red chard (both €5). They also host table quizzes, tastings and free food matching events. See their website and blog (mulligangrocer.blogspot.com) for more information.

- Starters: €5-7.50
- Mains: €12.50-16
- House Wine: €22

OPENING: From 2pm: Sat-Sun. From 4pm: Mon-Fri

**BOOKING:** Tel: 670 9889, email: table@lmulligangrocer.com

# LA MAISON

15 Castle Market Street, Dublin 2.

www.lamaisonrestaurant.ie

**D**on't let the fact that an episode of *Fade Street* was once filmed outside here put you off. On arrival at La Maison, if you can possibly wangle it, try to nab the table for two outdoors on the left which looks on to Castle Market. It is, quite simply, the most perfect people-watching vantage point in the whole city as both members of your party will have a birds' eye view of this particularly charming street. This makes it an ideal location for first dates or boring dinner guests who will need distraction. Even in winter it's a nice spot to nab as the staff will provide you with a little blanket if you sit outside. If, however, you're placed inside, rest assured this won't detract from your dining experience, as entering La Maison feels like you may have stepped into a little restaurant in gay Paris. Food here is classic French country fayre, best consumed at a leisurely pace. If you're there with a carnivorous paramour we'd recommend starting with one of their homemade patês (they change daily, €9.00) then split the cote de boeuf, which is rib of Irish beef served with salted potatoes and salad (€58) and finish by splitting the tarte tatin with apple sorbet (€13.50). Hopefully he doesn't split the bill though...

- Starters: €5.70-12.50
- Mains: €16.50-29
- House Wine: €24

OPENING: Lunch: Mon-Sun
Dinner: Mon-Sun

**BOOKING:** 672 7258

# LENNOX CAFE BISTRO

31 Lennox Street,
Dublin 8.

Okay, apparently Lennox hire each and every one of their staff from the latest Burberry campaign (swoon city). But we don't just go there to perv. We are also attracted by the eggs, the glorious eggs. Lennox does good brunch and everyone seems to know it – expect mega queues at the weekends, which are largely comprised of fabulously attractive young couples with their trendy prams. Fortunately, the waiting time has reduced dramatically since they expanded upstairs. Still, aim for a table downstairs, as we find those gorgeous staff may forget about you from time to time – not good fun with a hangover. Worth the trek to Portobello, we also highly recommend a stop in the Lower Deck on your way home (or indeed on the way to) for a cheeky pint/hair of the dog. But back to those eggs, oh those eggs. How do they get the poach so perfect every time? You must try their eggs benedict (€9.50), which are one of the best in town. Then there's the beef burger with crispy onions, smoked bacon and cheddar (€12.95) that'll have you belly-full all day. A perfect spot to be soothed by at the weekend, with the eye-candy waiting staff a pleasant bonus.

- Starters: €6.50-14.95
- Mains: €11.50-14.95
- House Wine: €19.95

OPENING: Lunch: Mon-Sun
Dinner: Mon-Sun

**BOOKING:** Tel: 478 9966

# LITTLE JERUSALEM

3 Wynnefield Road,
Rathmines, Dublin 6.

In the fashion of the Little Tokyos, Little Indias and Little Italys of other major cities, Dublin once had an enclave known as 'Little Jerusalem' in the area west of Portobello to Leonard's Corner (where South Circular Road and Clanbrassil Street meet). Though many of the immigrants who once populated this area have dispersed to the US and Israel; the local synagogues, schools and shops have closed and much of what had been a culturally-rich area has since quelled, another Little Jerusalem is rekindling the flame nearby. This Little Jerusalem, which serves up a delectable selection of Lebanese and Palestinian dishes, has no pretences about it, and it is what it is – little. So if you're expecting a palace and find yourself disappointed, it's your own fault. Abraham Phelan (the man at the helm, conveniently born just outside of Jerusalem) has made it clear that he really knows a thing or two about quality baba ganoush (an earthy dish of smoky aubergine) and falafel (savoury balls of deep-fried chickpeas and spice). You could have a complete satisfying meal for under €20 too, which is part of the appeal, but note that this doesn't include any alcoholic beverages. This place is BYOB – something we're fine with.

- Starters: €3.99-6.99
- Mains: €9.50-14.99
- House Wine: BYOB

OPENING: Dinner: Tues-Sun

**BOOKING:** 412 6912

# LOCKS BRASSERIE

1 Windsor Terrace,
Portobello, Dublin 8.
www.locksbrasserie.com

**T**his is a new restaurant with an old name – at least the third incarnation of Locks to reside on the Grand Canal and arguably the best. Sebastiaen Masi and Kirsten Batt decided to branch out after 10 years at Pearl Brasserie and opened this dapper dining room last year. They declared that their mission was to bring the same standard of good food and comfortable service enjoyed at Pearl to their new project. We can report it has been a case of so far, so good, due largely to the skills of head chef Rory Carville in the kitchen. He landed here via the Four Seasons and L'Ecrivain where he had already caught the eye of a number of restaurant critics, earning rave reviews for his rich and imaginative cooking. The view out to the canal, occasionally enlivened by a local character drinking al fresco on a nearby bench, can be pretty in the right light. There is an excellent private dining room upstairs, perfect for a special dinner with about nine of your favourite people. The best dish on the menu is a stuffed loin of rabbit served with confit leg pasilla, salsify purée, curly kale and black pepper emulsion for €25 – a truly delightful construction.

- Starters: €6-15
- Mains: €16-27
- House Wine: €24

OPENING: Lunch: Thu-Sun
Dinner: Mon-Sun

**BOOKING:** 420 0555, www.locksbrasserie.com

# LOUIE'S

20 Mountjoy Square
East,
Dublin 1.

www.louies.ie

Situated on the furthest reaches of Mountjoy Square (next stop, Croke Park), Louie's is a brave, trailblazing restaurant in an area of the city that's sadly bereft of as many decent eateries as a Southside equivalent. Under the helm of owner Tony Olin, it has become a favoured spot of Northsiders with a discerning palate, for many charming reasons. There's something very welcoming about the subterranean dining room that is tastefully kitted out with Tiffany lamps and amply-sized marble-topped tables, spaced far enough apart so you can discuss all kinds of matters without fear that you might be overheard by those next to you. We're also huge fans of their pre-theatre menu. For just €24.95 you can indulge in three delightful courses that you may savour at your leisure, as you're never rushed out of the place – at one meal, we were the last people there, and even then they didn't hover. Finally, the service is always impeccable. They hosted their first wedding there this year, and say they "felt it showed Louie's at its finest." We certainly can't imagine it being anything other than delightful. Chapter One should keep an eye on this place. It's quite the contender.

- Starters: €5.50-7.50
- Mains: €15.75-28
- House Wine: €21.50

OPENING: Lunch: Mon-Sun
Dinner: Wed-Sat

**BOOKING:** 836 4588, email: reservations@louies.ie

# MARCO PIERRE WHITE

51 Dawson Street,
Dublin 2.
www.marcopierrewhite.ie

At the end of his meal in Marco Pierre White's, Oscar winner Cuba Gooding Junior gave the food a standing ovation. Such is the quality of the grub dished up by Marco and his crew. However, if he'd also roared "show me the money" at the top of his voice to the bodyguard who was taking care of his wallet we wouldn't have been surprised, as prices here can tend toward the steep. But this doesn't seem to have dampened this restaurant's popularity; in fact, if anything, patrons seem happy to pay that little extra for the taste of luxury and ambient atmosphere that the darkened dining room offers. Mainly on special occasions, it must be said. Vegetarians, members of Weight Watchers and those with heart complaints would probably be advised to go elsewhere as cream, butter and red meat are the backbone of this restaurant. You can choose from rib-eye, fillet or T-bone when selecting your cut, which can then be paired with one of their classic accompaniments ranging from Bearnaise sauce (€30 when alongside a fillet steak) to Boston style, which has poivre noir and grilled oysters perched atop (€35 when smothering a T-Bone steak). And ne'er a Knorr beef stockpot in sight.

- Starters: €8.95-14.50
- Mains: €19.95-35
- House Wine: €24

OPENING: Lunch: Mon-Sun
Dinner: Mon-Sun

**BOOKING:** Tel: 677 1155, email: eat@marcopierrewhite.ie

# MATT THE THRESHER

31-32 Lower Pembroke Street, Dublin 2.
*www.matththresher.ie*

**NEW ENTRY**

The cut-out figure that stood outside The Pembroke pub still keeps watch at the door of this new seafood bar and grill. It is one of the few reminders of the mediocre drinking den for the Baggotonia office set that was here before Jimmy and Charlotte Lyons reinvented the venue with the help of chef Stephen Caviston. A sister to the restaurant of the same name in Tipperary, Matt's is busy at lunchtime when portions of beer-battered haddock and chunky chips with pureed peas (€12.95) are enthusiastically scoffed. Evening specials include grilled plaice in herb butter, side salad, baby potatoes and a glass of Hout Bay Sauvignon Blanc (€19.95). Caviston tells us one of his favourite ingredients to work with is fresh mackerel, so look out for this featuring amongst the daily specials when it's in season. During rare spells of sunshine we enjoy sitting at a table out front with a glass of Guinness and a portion of six Carlingford Rock oysters (€10). Sommelier Justin O'Hanlon leads regular wine-tasting evenings which utilises the well-appointed bar counter in the main room. There's an excellent pianist who occasionally plays live backing music to your meal, but we discovered after a recent boozy lunch that he doesn't take requests.

- Starters: €5.95-13.95
- Mains: €10.95-30
- House Wine: €20

OPENING: Lunch: Mon-Sat
Dinner: Mon-Sat

**BOOKING:** 676 2980

# McHUGH'S WINE & DINE

59 Saint Assam's Park
Dublin 5.
www.mchughs.ie/dine

The name of this restaurant does not inspire confidence – the fact that this bistro feels the need to confirm the presence of food and drink in bold lettering above the door seems unnecessary. However, we're delighted to report that the menu here is packed with interesting combinations, wonderfully executed. The modern interior is spacious, bright and comfortable – if a bit generic. We were impressed with the crumbed lamb breast starter, served with a delicious black olive puree, caper and parsley dressing (€8.60). A lighter but equally satisfying option would be chickpea falafels, pickled cucumber and spiced mint yoghurt for €6.50. The seared haunch of Glenmalure venison with roast turnip, colcannon mash, braised red cabbage with red wine jus (€17.90) will be satisfying for anyone with a predilection for hearty Irish dishes. Look out for the early bird menu offering two courses for €19 or three courses for €23. Owners Cathal and Diarmuid McHugh have been in the wine game for 16 years, so unsurprisingly there are some exciting bottles available here, and we highly recommend the Spanish Marques de Riscal Tempranillo, Castilla y León 2007 for €21.

● Starters: €4.75-8.60
● Mains: €13.50-23.95
● House Wine: €18

OPENING: Lunch: Mon-Sun
Dinner: Mon-Sun

**BOOKING:** 832 7435, email: dine@mchughs.ie

# MICHIE SUSHI

11 Chelmsford Lane,
Ranelagh, Dublin 6.
www.michiesushi.com

**Q**uestion: Where the hell can I find decent sushi in Dublin? Answer: In Ranelagh's Michie Sushi. This blink-and-you'll-miss-it eatery primarily trades on its popular take-out service for the well-heeled sushi-ites of D6, but don't be put off by the (very) tiny dining room – Michie does very good sushi. Fresh fish, perfect rice and ridiculously delicious sashimi make up for the fact that you can sometimes clearly hear the conversations the kitchen staff are having. If you do get a table (we got a nice little one by the window), it can be a nice snug space for a pair of close friends or a low-maintenance, casual date. But please note – do not go here if you are having a row with a loved one or dining with a boring colleague – the silence will make you lose the will to live no matter how good the sushi is. The ura maki combo at €9 is perfect for lunch, and the salmon and tuna combo for €12.50 is filling and delicious. Staff dress in kimonos and are very attentive (we get the feeling they'd be this way even if it wasn't such a small space). It's all dainty, fresh and precise – what makes sushi great, really.

- Sushi: €1.80-15
- House Wine: €13.50

OPENING: Tues-Sun:
12noon-10pm

**BOOKING:** 497 6438

# MOLOUGHNEY'S OF CLONTARF

9 Vernon Avenue,
Clontarf, Dublin 3.
www.molougneys.ie

**NEW ENTRY**

**W**e really do like an awful lot about this place. Decorative features such as exposed beams and high ceilings make it, dare we say, 'rustic', but in the best possible sense of that oft-abused word. Staff are smiley and attentive, but not at all pushy. And the wine list is a gem, with lots of good value bottles of decent stuff for around €20 to €30. But what really stands out here is the mind-bending menu (we guarantee you will want to order absolutely everything on it), the delightful dishes of which boast ingredients from some of our favourite Irish artisan producers. Special mention must go to the starter salad of roasted red and golden beetroot, fennel and St Tola goats' cheese, as it is an utter symphony on the tongue (€8.50). They care about sourcing Irish products and making seasonal and local choices. Even their hot smoked salmon is from their own smokery. Just beware the overwhelming portions on some of the main courses, especially if you're heading out afterwards; their enormity may leave you wanting to snuggle up with a duvet. The deal for two people (two courses and a bottle of wine for €55) is a winner. Oh, and their breakfast is delicious.

- Starters: €5.50-10
- Mains: €10.90-29.90
- House Wine: €19

OPENING: B/Fast & Lunch: Mon-Sun, Dinner: Tues-Sun

**BOOKING: 833 0002**

# MULBERRY GARDEN

Mulberry Lane, Donnybrook
Dublin 4
www.mulberrygarden.ie

**NEW ENTRY**

**M**ulberry Lane sounds pastoral, idyllic even. It's not. Mulberry Lane is a slightly scruffy suburban alley starting alongside Kielys pub in Donnybrook and meandering past some artisan housing. Look out for the sign to guide you towards the more appealing gastronomic oasis of Mulberry Garden. As you go indoors there's a small, plush bar on the left-hand side and, in front of you, the L-shaped dining room with plain-ish but tasteful decor, the battleship-grey walls relieved by a mural of stretched purple yarn. The menu, presented on printed slips of paper, changes weekly – which brings us to the twist in this tale. In some ways, you could consider Mulberry Garden the most ambitious and accomplished pop-up restaurant in the city. They only open for dinner on Thursday, Friday and Saturday, where they serve a three-course meal for €40, with two options for each course. This concept, brought to you by the team behind Eatery 120, won't be to everyone's taste, but we have been delighted by the adventure of tucking into an array of dishes prepared by the chefs based on ingredients sourced from Dublin markets. There is a yin-yang vibe to the food, everything in balance with picture-perfect presentation. Check their website for what treats are available this week.

- 3 course dinner: €40
- House Wine: €22

OPENING: Dinner: Thurs-Sat

**BOOKING:** 269 3300, email: eat@mulberrygarden.ie

# NONNA VALENTINA

1 Portobello Road,
Dublin 8.
*www.nonnavalentina.ie*

**F**ans of the Dublin-wide Italian eateries Dunne & Crescenzi, owned by romantic and business partners, Eileen and Stefan, will be glad to hear that they also offer a more upmarket dining experience in Portobello. Nonna Valentina is named after Stefan's grandmother, whose recipe book inspired the menu. This is authentic Italian home cooking served with Crescenzi's signature flair. The antipasti showcases some of Italy's finest produce, including prosciutto from San Daniele and buffalo mozzarella from Campania (Nonna's famous bruschetta, drizzled with extra virgin olive oil from Lazio, is a firm favourite); while pasta fans will appreciate the break from the norm. They've eschewed penne and spaghetti in favour of squid ink tagliolini and tonnarelli. There's also a nod to Irish cuisine with pork, lamb cutlets and venison served with an Italian twist. And make sure to leave room for dessert – their panna cotta is nothing short of spectacular. Nonna Valentina, like its canal-mate Locks, is a true neighbourhood restaurant. The Portobello set dine here *en masse*, which lends conviviality – and often a spot of divilment – to proceedings. By the same token, its peaceful setting overlooking the Grand Canal makes it a surefire spot for romantic rendezvous. *Buon appetito!*

- Starters: €6.50-11.00
- Mains: €14.50-25
- House Wine: €18

OPENING: Lunch: Sat-Sun
Dinner: Tues-Sun

**BOOKING:** 454 9866, www.nonnavalentina.ie

# NOSHINGTON

186 South
Circular Road,
Dublin 8.

**NEW ENTRY**

Noshington lies at the top of Washington Street just off the South Circular Road, hence the pithy name. It is exactly the kind of subdued, friendly, relaxed neighbourhood hangout that anyone would want to live beside. Inside is a modest array of modern chairs and tables, and out back is a recently opened garden terrace, laid out with cute tables and chairs slightly reminiscent of junior infants. If the weather is kind, this is a pleasant secluded corner for a lazy lunch. When we visit, our waitress invariably introduces the menu with zeal. They are enthusiastic about what they do here, in a cool way. They have a mixed-up menu really, some Middle Eastern influence – one of the chefs is Palestinian – with a few of the expected salad combos and the obligatory soup and a sandwich option. All relatively cheap. Try the spicy lamb burger with tzatziki and roasted sweet potato (€10), a filling bundle of flavour – comfort food to get excited about. We recently enjoyed a daily special mixed salad with a mustard dressing, Toulouse sausage and topped off with a poached egg – a steal at €8 – washed down with a chilled bottle of their Montesierra Rose (€17.50). Shane MacGowan is a regular.

- Mains: €6-11.50
- House Wine: €17.50

OPENING: Lunch: Tues-Sun

**BOOKING:** 410 0414

# O'CONNELL'S

135 Morehampton Rd,
Donnybrook,
Dublin 4.

www.oconnellsdonnybrook.com

**NEW ENTRY**

**D**onnybrook has seen some delightful additions to its restaurant landscape of late. The brilliant Mulberry Garden is also in this top 100, and O'Connell's is another beauty. Located in what was formerly Madigan's pub, where RTÉ folk oft imbibed, it is the work of Tom O'Connell, brother of our original celebrity chef, Darina Allen. Tom moved to O'Connell's from Bewley's Hotel to The Berkeley before settling in Donnybrook, and we hope he stays, as this menu has so many gorgeous offerings. He keeps it simple; the ethos of clan O'Connell and the Allens being fresh ingredients, cooked well at keen prices. So you leave content of both belly and wallet. It's a far cry from #deepfriedchickenclubtikkagoujon pub fare, and will satisfy the most discerning of post-match Leinster fans. It's also perfect if your parents are in town of a Sunday. The family thing is big business here though – so avoid for a date night. The fish dishes are great and their steak is something to write home about. But most divine are the very cute, and very clever Little Pot Desserts (€6.95 for a choice of two per person), which will have you dribbling and using words like, 'luscious' and 'exquisite' with abandon.

- Starters: €6.95-9
- Mains: €16.50-27.25
- House Wine: €22.50

OPENING: Lunch: Mon-Sun
Dinner: Mon-Sun

**BOOKING:** 269 6116/269 6125, email: info@oconnellsdonnybrook.com

# ODESSA

13 Dame Court,
Dublin 2.

*www.odessa.ie*

We remember when the Odessa club was one of those exclusive places where not 'just anybody' could make it inside. That was then, and this is now... we are where we are... recessionary times... and so on and so forth... yawn. So now, exclusivity quashed and egalitarianism enshrined, even its restaurant seems to be gaining wider reception – as some wise person once said, "What better way to appeal to the general public than by granting accessibility to the general public?" Amen to that. Last time we wrote about this hot spot, we raved about the Fivers menu, which is really excellent value, and the items off the Soul Food section of the menu (the grilled jerk chicken has been a long-time favourite, delicious). Though they're still proving popular, it's the brunch menu that seems to have folks raving again these days, with huevos rancheros for €11 and eggs florentine for the same price. We tend to agree. We'll never tire of the classic Odessa burger with smoked applewood cheese (€14), and if you wanted to go for their much-talked-about chicken quesadilla with guacamole and lime tequila dressing (€16), we certainly wouldn't advise against it.

- Starters: €4.50-7.50
- Mains: €14-28.50
- House Wine: €21.50

OPENING: Lunch: Mon-Sun
Dinner: Mon-Sun

**BOOKING:** Tel: 670 7634, email: info@odessa.ie

# OLIVIER'S @ THE SCHOOL HOUSE

2-8 Northumberland Road
Ballsbridge, Dublin 4.

*www.oliviers.ie*

**NEW ENTRY**

If you were still wondering exactly which 'Ollie' to thank for this elegant contribution from The Schoolhouse Hotel in Ballsbridge, it's Breton chef Olivier Quenet of French smash-hit La Maison, a restaurant that seems to have brought together more restaurant staff (from other restaurants) than any other. They must be doing something right. Olivier has not only been spreading smiles with this similarly French-inspired menu, he's also substantially upped the creativity stakes for rival restaurants (and the enjoyment stakes for diners) by hosting a number of themed events such as a whiskey-inspired menu, and 'Spirited Away', a cocktail-themed menu. Pop in for lunch, a drink – whatever you feel like on the day. And it's not just the fancy that the wonderful Olivier specialises in; being the multi-talented man that he is, he's also a pro at all things simple. Who'd have thought a chicken or beef and Guinness pot pie (€14.50) or a lamb stew (also €14.40) could be so good? Granted they are bistro menu stalwarts, but you won't find better in Dublin. Lunch set price menu is €22 for a two-course and €27 for three. Pre-theatre is €35 for three courses, 6pm-7pm.

- Starters: €7.50-16
- Mains: €17-49.50
- House Wine: €24

**OPENING:** Lunch: Tues-Fri
Dinner: Tues-Sat

**BOOKING:** 6675014, email: aisling@schoolhousehotel.com

# ONE PICO

5-6 Molesworth Place,
Dubin 2.

www.onepico.com

Former wunderkind of Irish restaurants, Eamonn O'Reilly, opened One Pico when he was just 25. Fifteen years later it is still going from strength to strength, while the chef/restauranteur at its helm has added many more strings to his bow, including the Box Tree in Stepaside (a new entry in this year's guide). One Pico is old-school fancy, but a recent refurbishment has attracted a younger demographic. Where once the clientele was almost entirely made up of Dublin's well heeled over-40s; you're now just as likely to find sybaritic 20-somethings enjoying O'Reilly's creations. The food is consistently good (as the awards will testify), but if you want specific suggestions we recommend the langoustine risotto: sautéed Dublin Bay prawns, truffle bisque, sweet peas and sorrel (€16.50) and the exquisite combination of seared scallops and crisp rare breed pork belly, with cauliflower puree (€31). In the words of the man himself: "all our customers are VIPs", but if you fancy some rubber-necking after your belly-filling, you may spot the likes of Bono, Enda Kenny and Brendan Gleeson. Should you not have a celebrity bank balance like theirs, opt for the €24 lunch menu, which is refreshingly lacking in the sneaky supplements favoured by too many top-tier restaurants.

- Starters: €12-18
- Mains: €24-34
- House Wine: €26

OPENING: Lunch: Mon-Sun
Dinner: Mon-Sun

BOOKING: Tel: 676 0300

# OUZO'S

22 Castle Street, Dalkey &
Main Street, Blackrock

*www.ouzos.ie*

**NEW ENTRY**

**O**uzos has bucked the economic trend. While many restaurants have pulled down their shutters, Ouzo's have flung open the doors of another restaurant in Blackrock. Menu-wise, the second incarnation is a near replica to the Dalkey outpost. The focus is on quality steak and seafood at reasonable prices. They are passionate about using Irish produce and they champion suppliers such as master butcher Pat Caulfield who provides their dry-aged steaks – always a good sign. Ouzos keep their dishes simple, relying on fresh produce rather than pomp and ceremony. We hasten to add that they have their own fishing boat – the Golden Venture – and land all their own crab and lobster. 'Surf and turf' is, in theory, such an easy dish, but the quality of the produce often lets it down. Ouzos' version is spot on. The *piece de resistance*, however, is the Great Crab and Lobster Feast, €59.95 for two including a bottle of house wine. The two-courser allows patrons to enjoy a crab starter and a lobster main (which they can pick from the tank). They also offer a Sunday lunch menu starting at €17.95 for two courses, and €22.95 for three courses. Ouzos really do offer that rare thing: remarkable food at reasonable prices.

- Starters: €4.50-9.95
- Mains:  €14.95-24.95
- House Wine:  €19.95

OPENING: Lunch: Mon-Sun
Dinner: Mon-Sun

**BOOKING:** (Dalkey) 285 1890, (Blackrock) 210 1000, email: reservations@ouzos.

# PACINO'S

18 Suffolk Street,
Dublin 2.
www.pacinos.ie

**NEW ENTRY**

I t is simple really. Serve up reasonably-priced pizza, put it together with cold beer and you have a guaranteed a crowd-pleasing formula. Dublin is littered with restaurants that dish out stodgy bases and scorched toppings, but decent pizza joints are few and far between. Just off Grafton Street, however, Pacino's is building up a reputation for some winning combinations, and exploiting its versatile venue for everything from singles' nights to salsa classes. Try the house special pizza, which comes topped with a generous selection of black olives, ham, peppers, pepperoni and mushrooms. A 10" serving is €11.95, and a 12" €13.95. If you are a bit more adventurous – or just more indecisive – you can order a Quattro Stagioni, a pizza topped in four sections with parma ham, artichoke, smoked salmon and beef tomato with parmesan shavings (€14.95 for 12").

There is an early bird menu, but Pacino's caters specifically for night owls on a Friday and Saturday, opening till 2.30am. Look out for regular live music, take a cute hipster with you, or pick one up when you get there. Incidentally, when the cast of television restaurant drama *Raw* finish filming, this is where they choose for their wrap party meal.

- Starters: €2.95-10
- Mains: €9.95-25.95
- House Wine: €26

OPENING: Lunch: Mon-Sun
Dinner: Mon-Sun

**BOOKING:** Tel: 677 5651, www.pacinos.ie

# PAULIE'S PIZZA

58 Grand Canal Street,
Dublin 4.

www.juniors.ie

Juniors or Paulie's, Juniors or Paulie's... It's hard to decide which of these two restaurants from the McNerney brothers we like more. Since opening in 2010, this pizza joint has rapidly built a dedicated band of diners who enjoy their brisk service, buzzy atmosphere and authentic food – the wood fired pizza oven was imported specially from Italy. While they also serve pasta, we'd recommend heading straight for the pizza part of the menu for maximum satisfaction. Try the super picante, which consists of spicy salami, fresh chilli, red peppers, rocket, tomato and smoked mozzarella (€15). Yes, it's hot, so maybe not for the faint-hearted. They only take reservations on the day and it can get very busy at the weekends, leading to a bit of a wait. As there is nothing like a few beers to make pizza taste all the better, we'd recommend getting your name on the list at the door as early as you can and then mooching off to Slattery's for a bit of a pre-dinner drink (they'll ring when they're ready for you.) Ladies take note, Jamie Heaslip has admitted he is a fan. Just in case you'd lose the run of yourself if you saw him there, we thought we'd warn you.

- Starters: €7-10
- Mains: €14-18
- House Wine: €20

OPENING: Dinner: Tues-Sun

**BOOKING:** On the day, telephone 664 3658

■ 100

# PEARL BRASSERIE

20 Merrion Street Upper,
Dublin 2.

www.pearl-brasserie.com

**P**earl should have a warning upon reservation. If you are lucky enough to get a booth, you are probably going to fall in love with your date and leave choosing which school your kids should go to. It has been known to happen. But whether the romance lasts, the love affair with Pearl is for life. One of our preferred dining spaces in the city, Pearl's food is the mastercraft of its chef Sébastien Masi. His French cuisine involves exciting and impeccable food with careful seasonal touches. If you can tear yourself away from our favourite of the squab pigeon rossini – cooked two ways, black truffle mousseline and pan-fried duck foie gras (€30) – go for one of the specials. Even if you're what they call a 'safe eater', choosing one at random has always been a risk that pays off. It's the type of white linen-adorned table establishment that can resolve any problem and heal any heartache with their fine food and soft lighting. You'll really have to leave it all behind if you want to enter this space. Just don't blame them if you do happen to swing up the stairs and hear Dean Martin singing "...that's *amore*..." You'll likely feel like singing too.

- Starters: €8-18
- Mains: €19-30
- House Wine: €28

**OPENING:** Lunch: Mon-Fri
Dinner: Mon-Sat

**BOOKING:** Tel: 661 3572, email: info@pearl-brasserie.com

# PEPLOE'S

16 St Stephen's Green,
Dublin 2.

www.peploes.com

There is something about Peploe's that makes you feel that you've been granted access to a members-only club. Perhaps it's because of its location in the basement of a Georgian house on leafy St. Stephen's Green; perhaps it's because of the charming front-of-house staff who give the impression that a foot massage wouldn't be out of the question. Either way, you feel like you've stepped over a red velvet rope as you're led to your table. Peploe's has always attracted a monied crowd (both locals and tourists from the nearby five-star hotels). Ergo, people-watching is the preferred sport (eating and drinking take a close second). The menu spans the globe, with wild mushroom bruschetta for Italophiles, a Gallic-inspired French onion soup, as well as some closer-to-home offerings such as wild rabbit risotto and Irish fillet steak. If you had to give it a bracket, it would be 'bistro-style comfort food'. Decent portions take precedence over poncey bisques and foams. Be warned, though, the Peploe's cottage pie (€13.50), served during lunchtime, and homemade prawn ravioli are so comforting that they may actually induce sleep. For value, try the pre-concert dinner (€25 for three courses), which is complemented by a menu of good value, and well considered, wines by the glass.

- Starters: €6.25-14.50
- Mains: €19.50-29.50
- House Wine: €24

OPENING: Lunch: Mon-Fri
Dinner: Mon-Sat

**BOOKING:** Tel: 676 3144

# THE PIG'S EAR

4 Nassau Street,
Dublin 2.

*www.thepigsear.ie*

**NEW ENTRY**

**G**etting a table at the window in The Pig's Ear is a real treat. While that's not to say your meal will suffer if you're at one of the other tables, it simply must be said that beside one of their gorgeous Georgian windows, the dining experience is enhanced as you look down at the crowds on Nassau Street and across into Trinity College, and breathe in the atmosphere of a dusky Dublin evening. Indeed, it also makes the rather arduous ascent to the first floor even more worthwhile. Inside, there's also a feeling of history as they serve up their brand of Irish cookery that gives a subtle nod to the food that your Granny might make, only here it's a turbo-charged version. The interior is a delight; rustic wooden boards, Kilner jars and antique looking casserole dishes abound. They're famed for their shepherd's pie (€18.95), but we suggest you try their brown bread ice cream with crushed yellow man (€7.95). Bargain hunters should try their early evening menu (three courses for €24.95) and the restaurant is within an easy walk of most of the city's theatres. However, we would recommend walking to the theatre, no one wants to succumb to a food coma midway through a first act.

- Starters: €6.95-10.95
- Mains: €17.95-26.95
- House Wine: €20.95

OPENING: Lunch: Mon-Sat
Dinner: Mon-Sat

**BOOKING:** 670 3865

# PINOCCHIO

Luas Kiosk,
Ranelagh, Dublin 6.

*www.pinocchiodublin.ie*

**P**inocchio occupies an unusual location at the Luas kiosk in Ranelagh. Ordinarily, a space like this would house a newsagent or coffee shop, not a high-end Italian trattoria. Yet somehow it works. Despite the modern façade of the building – all glass and steel – the interior is totally authentic. Think low lighting, exposed wine cellars and Italian paraphernalia. The only suggestion that you are positioned below a tram stop is the occasional whoosh of a passing carriage overhead. The passion that the all-Italian team have for their operation is obvious - they also run an Italian cookery school and travel company. What's more, the cured meats (which are cut in front of you), cheeses and olive oils are all directly imported, and you really can taste the difference. We're fans of the spaghetti allo scoglio (€15.50) and the lasagnetta al ragu' di agnello menta e cioccolato (€14.90), and yes, that translates to lasagne with chocolate (trust us, it works). Otherwise, their value menu of two courses for €19.90 offers extensive choice. Their coffee is also noteworthy, and thankfully they sell it for home brewing, along with all sorts of other gourmet goodies that Italophiles will drool over. Finding better Italian food than this will involve an air fare.

- Starters: €5.50-12
- Mains: €14.50-22
- House Wine: €20

OPENING: Lunch: Mon-Sun
Dinner: Mon-Sun

**BOOKING:** Tel: 497 0111, email: info@pinocchio.ie

# THE PORT HOUSE

64 South William Street
Dublin 2.
www.porthouse.ie

**NEW ENTRY**

The biggest problem with The Port House is not knowing when to stop when ordering from their menu of delightful little tapas dishes. More often than not, your eye is bigger than your belly and with a lot of food left on the table, you realise you simply can't squeeze in another morsel. We give you this warning because their candle-lit surroundings are perfect for a romantic date, and we wouldn't want you to make a pig of yourself in front of your future spouse. Happily, the friendly, knowledgeable staff can guide you against going overboard, and can suggest a wine or something from their exclusive selection of port that should prove the perfect accompaniment to your meal. They also serve until closing at midnight, lest you want to dine late or linger on over a few extra glasses. Our favourite dish is the chorizo al vino, chorizo sausage in red wine (€6.30) – mopping up the sauce from this dish with a hunk of their delicious bread is certainly not frowned upon, but positively encouraged. Feeling brave? Try their speciality of pulpo al Gallego (€10.65), which is octopus Gallician style finished in extra virgin olive oil, sea salt and sweet smoked paprika.

- Tapas: €2.90-14.50
- House Wine: €23

OPENING: Lunch: Mon-Sun
Dinner: Mon-Sun

**BOOKING:** Tel: 677 0298 (Parties of 10+)

# IL PRIMO

16 Montague Street,
Dublin 2.

www.ilprimo.ie

Il Primo turned 20 years old this year, making it one of Dublin's longest-established Italian dining institutions. But just because it's no longer a teenager doesn't mean that there's any less fun to be had during a visit to this restaurant. The extensive selection of carefully considered Tuscan wines may have something to do with that... The menu is also of the Tuscan variety - rustic and unadorned, chef Anita Thoma lets the fresh ingredients do the talking. For our money, the risotto and pasta (the fresh pasta is made on site) dishes are some of the best in Dublin. The signature dish, however, has to be the crab, lemon and leek lasagne (€18), which, in true Italian tradition, can also be enjoyed as a primi piatti for €10. A word to the wise: the pizzas come *sans* cheese, another Italian tradition that not everyone will enjoy.

Il Primo occupies a charming little period house tucked away on Montague Street (between Harcourt Street and Wexford Street). It's a small but perfectly formed establishment that feels instantly welcoming. We are particular fans of their *al fresco* seating area during the summer months, if you're lucky enough to snag a table that is. The perfect spot to while away an afternoon.

- Starters: €9-10
- Mains: €16-24
- House Wine: €23

OPENING: Lunch: Mon-Fri
Dinner: Mon-Sat

**BOOKING:** Tel: 478 3373

# RASAM

18-19 Glasthule Road,
Glasthule,
Co. Dublin.
www.rasam.ie

When the much-admired and well respected Nisheeth Tak and Rangan Arulchelvan opened this restaurant above The Eagle House pub in Glasthule eight years ago, they probably weren't anticipating acquiring regulars such as Pat Kenny, Chris De Burgh and Neil Jordan. Perhaps it's the contribution of these folks that has led to the wild success of the place (they're opening another branch in January of 2012), but we'll wager not; word on the street is that within days of opening, their lamb curry (the lal maas, €18.95) reached near-mythical status. 'Sounds crazy,' we hear you say. Well, you simply won't know until you try it. We'd be lying if we said it didn't change our standards. Another major contender in the Dublin Indian culinary scene is the mansahari thali – a mouth-watering selection of prawn, lamb, chicken and dal, and spinach served with pulao, naan and homemade pickles. Our only complaint is that there's a lot of it, and the fact that it's so tasty means there's a chance you'll eat it till you're in severe pain (especially if you've helped yourself to some starters – we did). It definitely would not hurt to share it, and at €27.50, it's an absolute steal to split.

- Starters: €6.95-15.95
- Mains: €16.95-27.50
- House Wine: €19.95

OPENING: Dinner: Mon-Sun

**BOOKING:** Tel: 230 0600

Santa Rita
RESERVA

SINCE 1880

CABERNET SAUV

D.O. VALLE DEL MAIPO - C

**Enjoy SANTA RITA Sensibly**
Visit drinkaware.ie

# RESIDENCE
## RESTAURANT FORTY ONE
41 St Stephen's Green
Dublin 2.
*www.residence.ie*

**T**his place is full of surprises. First, you should know that being a member of Residence isn't a prerequisite for entrance into Restaurant Forty One. Although based on the first floor of the Georgian private members club, any Joe Schmo from the street can stroll in and make a reservation. Comprised of two immaculately turned out rooms – there is an abundance of artful flower arrangements, pressed linen, nicely weighted cutlery and delicate bone china – RFO puts the fine into fine dining, both in terms of their cuisine and presentation. Food is traditional Irish in nature, but with a few individual twists and tweaks from its supremely-talented head chef Graham Neville, so Dinish Island scallops are there but accompanied by truffled onions and the rather exotic-sounding coral bisque (€21.20). Second surprising fact is that although exclusive and attracting a rather juicy clientele list – so juicy in fact we're not at liberty to name some of the big stars who go there – they have great offers to attract regular Dubliners. The set dinner menu is €67.50 for five courses including tea or coffee and petit fours, pre-theatre is €36.40 for three courses and lunch is just €28.90 for three courses. With food this good, that's a real bargain.

- Starters: €15.40-19.80
- Mains: €32.20-34.85
- House Wine: €28

OPENING: Lunch: Tues-Sat
Dinner: Tues-Sat

**BOOKING:** 662 0000, or email info@reisdence.ie

# RESTAURANT PATRICK GUILBAUD

21 Upper Merrion Street,
Dublin 2.

www.restaurantpatrickguilbaud.ie

In 2011, Patrick Guilbaud celebrated his 30th year in Dublin, and a book was published chronicling his restaurant's last three decades – in all its incarnations – bravely entitled *The First Thirty Years*. When he first arrived in 1981, the city was gripped by recession, so Guilbaud is well used to rolling with the fiscal punches and currently has some fantastic lunch deals on offer (which allows even the most financially embarrassed among us to sample his gastronomic wonders). This includes a two-course lunch for €36, and coming from a restaurant with two Michelin stars, it might just be one of Dublin's best-kept culinary secrets. Originally on St James' Place, Restaurant Patrick Guilbaud now calls Upper Merrion Street its home, and its dining room, which boasts an impressive collection of Irish art, ranks among the most remarkable in the country. These days you're more likely to find chef Guillaume Lebrun in the kitchen than Guilbaud himself, but the food, wine and service is always of the high standard we've come to expect. The tasting menu, which costs €90 for four courses (or eight courses for €165), reads like a last meal request from a foodie on death row. In fact, you'd kill for a taste.

- 2 courses: €85
- 3 courses: €105
- 4 courses: €130

OPENING: Lunch: Tues-Sat
Dinner: Tues-Sat

**BOOKING:** Tel: 676 4192

# RESTAURANT 1014

324 Clontarf Road,
Dublin 3.
www.restaurant1014.com

Owned by Margaret Butler and the Caring and Sharing Foundation, this young establishment has been making rather a few waves since it first opened as an upscale neighbourhood bistro two years ago. But this place is not just about sumptuous food (though you'd be foolish to not try their slow cooked pork belly, €20.95, which hits the spot every time for us). It's also not just about their critically acclaimed wines (you really should try the Château Haut Rian from Bordeaux, €14 for a half bottle) - there's more to it than all that. As you may have heard, they've recently opened a charity bookstore and tea room – which means you can have a nibble, a read and a sip while simultaneously contributing to a good cause. Also worth noting is the fact that they now serve breakfast from 10am every day (we can't resist their Out of the Oven fruit scones, €2.95 a piece) and a Table D'hote menu (starter and main for €19.95) six days a week. The only downside to their preparing the food right in front of you is that you'll have to exercise some serious willpower to not leap from your seat and snap it up before it's finished.

- Starters: €4.95-9.95
- Mains: €14.95-25.95
- House Wine: €20.95

OPENING: Lunch: Mon-Sun
Dinner: Mon-Sun

BOOKING: Tel: 805 4877, email: margaretbutler1014@gmail.com

# RIGBYS
## DELI & DINING ROOM

126 Upper Leeson Street, Dublin 4.

**NEW ENTRY**

James Rigby is an unusual, contrary chef. He doesn't like groups of men, and he doesn't like groups of women. He hates critics too, and reserves the right to chuck you out if he doesn't like you. There is no menu. There's a sign that says, "Take it or leave it." You eat what he feels like cooking, and he cooks it right in front of you. The place is tiny, you have to bring your own booze and the chances are you might not even get a table. It's all a bit *Fawlty Towers*. On our first visit, we asked if we could order the tomato soup and were told, "No chance. Absolutely no way." James Rigby may be temperamental, but he is also a deeply passionate chef who knows exactly what he's doing. What he does with wild sea bream is outrageous, and everything else we tasted was supremely good – especially the puddings. He might not care to charm you, but he cares deeply about whatever he chooses to put in front of you. So if you're in the mood to be doted on, have your ego built up or your ass kissed, you'll probably want to avoid this place. If you're just into your food, on the other hand, we heartily suggest that you rush to Rigbys.

- Starters: €6
- Mains: €15
- House Wine: BYOB

**OPENING:** Lunch: Mon-Sun
Dinner: Mon-Sun

**BOOKING:** Tel: 087 793 9195

# RUSTIC STONE

17 South Great Georges Street, Dublin 2.

www.rusticstone.ie

**R**ustic Stone isn't for everyone. If you've a real sweet tooth and believe no meal is complete without a hefty dose of sugar, salt or cream, you might be disappointed. Also, though the Stone opened to great praise a year ago, not everyone was pleased at their 'cook it yourself' ethos. We can see how after a long day at work you may not feel like cooking your own steak, but like we said, different strokes for different folks. Their fillet of beef with truffle chips at €35 seems to be flying off the (stone?), so we have to assume there's enough people out there who really dig it. We, personally, are into the emphasis on health and the menu is especially attractive if you don't eat wheat, gluten or dairy (some of us don't). With descriptions detailing the heath benefits of the dishes, the menu is unique.

We liked knowing that our starter of borlotti bean minestrone soup with chorizo (€6.95/€10.95 for a main) was full of protein and fibre with 'the most nutritious, chunky vegetables [proprietor Dylan McGrath] could find'. A tip: we prefer the seats upstairs because downstairs can get smoky at times – maybe that's just because the talented chefs are on fire (please pardon the pun), which indeed they are.

- **Starters:** €5.25-10.95
- **Mains:** €9.95-31
- **House Wine:** €20

**OPENING:** Lunch: Mon-Sat
Dinner: Mon-Sun

**BOOKING:** Tel: 707 9596

115 ∎

# THE SADDLE ROOM

27 St Stephen's Green,
Dublin 2.
www.theshelbourne.ie

**O**verlooking the largest garden square in the whole of Europe, our very own St Stephen's Green, is the Shelbourne Hotel, a significant landmark in Dublin since 1824 when it was purchased by Tipperary man Martin Burke. And for all you fact fans out there, room 112 was also where the first Irish Constitution was drafted in 1922. Sadly, it proved too difficult to fit a 135-seat restaurant into 'The Constitution Room' so instead, we have the grand Saddle Room on the ground floor. While The Saddle Room is indeed spacious and modern, the atmosphere is in keeping with the tradition of the Shelbourne and that's reflected in its dress code – requiring shirts and slacks, something that you don't hear much of these days. But once inside, the open kitchen and the oyster bar let us know we are very much in the 21st century, and if you manage to find yourself in The Saddle Room on a particularly busy evening, the mood is positively buzzing.

The menu offers a huge range of organic steak and a wide array of the freshest Irish seafood. For us, it's difficult not to go for the royal fish pie (€25.95) every time, but we promise we'll try the steaks some day (soon).

- Starters: €7.95-14.95
- Mains: €15-36
- House Wine: €27

**OPENING:** Lunch: Mon-Sun
Dinner: Mon-Sun

**BOOKING:** Tel: 663 4500, or book online

# SEAN MAC D'S

69 Harolds Cross Road,
Dublin 6
facebook.com/seanmacds

**NEW ENTRY**

**Y**ou'd be forgiven for thinking the most glamorous culinary delights available on this busy stretch of Harold's Cross Road would be a three-in-one or a batter burger, which was the case up until a year ago when Sean Mac D's gastropub opened. While it is still mainly a pub, the food on offer is of a much higher standard than your typical drinking emporium, with the likes of fresh Atlantic cod with mash, spinach, capers and sage on offer for a more than reasonable €14. And the fact that it's all made from scratch on the premises already puts it miles ahead of most of the other places serving food in the area. On special occasions (mainly Sundays around public holidays) a whole hog can be seen roasting on a spit in the smoking area, and if you pop your head into the garden you'll see four pet chickens (not available for eating) having a leisurely wander around. The pub itself is fairly typical, but some nice photographs and small art pieces on the wall make the whole place more inviting. The atmosphere is one of community spirit with Harold's Cross locals in the know frequenting the place. Some artisan and craft beers are available and kids eat free on Sundays.

- Starters: €3.50-8
- Mains: €10-16
- House Wine: €19.99

OPENING: Lunch: Mon-Sun
Dinner: Mon-Sun

**BOOKING:** Tel: 497 6832

# SEAPOINT

4 The Crescent,
Monkstown, Co. Dublin

www.seapointrestaurant.com

**NEW ENTRY**

Over the past few years it has been the local, suburban restaurants that have proved themselves to be the most innovative and exciting new eating experiences in our city, and Seapoint in Monkstown ranks among the finest of the out-of-town eateries. Since its opening just over three years ago, Seapoint has received glowing reviews from almost every publication in Dublin. Taking full advantage of its coastal location, the restaurant offers some of the freshest seafood our seas have to offer, with a menu that changes seasonally depending on what is available. If you find yourself there at the right time of year, we highly recommend the pan-roasted fillet of brill, sauteed spinach, saffron-poached baby potatoes with crispy pork belly and a mussel sauce (€23.50) which, for us, ticks all the boxes. The interiors, chosen by Eden Home & Garden in Blackrock, are nautically-themed and blend into their surroundings perfectly. The smokers among us are very happy to note that Seapoint also has a 'cigar menu' with excellent tasting notes that put most wine lists to shame. Finish the evening off with a relaxing walk along the pier to make it even more worth the trek.

- Starters: €7.50-12.50
- Mains: €17.50-28.50
- House Wine: €22.50

OPENING: Lunch: Mon-Sun
Dinner: Mon-Sat

---

**BOOKING:** 663 8480, www.seapointrestaurant.com

# THE TEA ROOM
## @ THE CLARENCE

6-8 Wellington Quay,
Dublin 2.
*www.theclarence.ie*

**NEW ENTRY**

The Tea Room remains one of the most impressive dining rooms in the city – bright, imposing and elegant. Notice the grainy black and white image of the old ballroom of The Clarence Hotel printed on the menu and you will realise that much of the original design remains. Modern touches include a collection of paintings by Guggi, an elevated bar and a banquette splitting the dining room. For most of its recent existence, this restaurant has been largely ignored by Dubliners, its tables sparsely populated by louche American visitors, clusters of conspiratorial businessmen and the occasional rock star. This is changing rapidly, particularly at lunch time where a two-course lunch for €16.50 or three courses for €19.50 has gained an enthusiastic following. Try the mushroom tortellini starter – delicate pasta parcels in a thick St Gall Farm House cheese fondue with balsamic vinegar and white truffle oil. We enjoyed the Fermanagh bacon steak served up with colcannon and parsley sauce. The standard of food is remarkable for these prices, and executive chef Mathieu Melin is a young star in the making. Make sure to pop into the hotel's Octagon bar after your meal. We're particularly partial to their Apple Strudel Martini (€9.50).

- Starters: €5.50-13.95
- Mains: €14.40-28
- House Wine: €19

OPENING: Lunch: Mon-Sun
Dinner: Mon-Sun

**BOOKING:** Tel: 407 0813, email: tearoom@theclarence.ie

# THORNTON'S

128 St. Stephen's Green,
Dublin 2.

www.thorntonsrestaurant.com

To say that Kevin Thornton produces food seems a bit gauche. Art is a more apt description of what has been coming out of his kitchen for the past 21 years. Furthermore, 'dinner' is far too dull a word to describe the quite incredible experience of eating there. Each visit is more akin to attending an epic performance where you have a front row seat. Kevin is nothing if not a perfectionist, so each dish brought to the table reeks of his genius (and yes, 'genius' is not to strong a word here). Unconvinced? Well consider the sea urchin dish he serves. It's only available as part of the tasting menu, and only if the urchin has been caught that day. That's the way Kevin rolls. And it's is not

- 3 courses: €76
- 5 course tasting: €90
- 8 course tasting: €120
- House Wine: €35

OPENING: Lunch: Thurs-Sat
Dinner: Tues-Sat

just plonked on a plate with a bit of sauce drizzled on the side, not on Kevin's watch. Instead it is brought to the table on a bed of beetroot salt and seaweed, which provides the scent of the ocean. It is then placed on a serving dish which billows out dry ice from underneath in imitation of a light sea mist, and just when you think he's nothing else up his sleeve, tiny speakers under the dish begin to play the sound of the ocean and gulls crying. Yep, it's not McDonalds.

**BOOKING:** Tel: 478 7008, email: thorntonsrestaurant@eircom.net

# TOWN BAR AND GRILL

21 Kildare St,
Dublin 2.
www.townbarandgrill.com

Town Bar and Grill is a favourite of the great and the good and has served dinner to many, many celebrities during its seven-year existence (think Michael Jordan, Christina Aguilera and Danny deVito, though not all on the same night). We of course include ourselves among these luminaries, as TbnG famously plays host to *The Dubliner*'s annual Christmas lunch, which is always a glittering affair (Chris de Burgh is never off the piano...). Now owned by Gillian Ronan, with Peter Murphy taking over in the kitchen, the high calibre of clientele still flock to Town 2.0, attracted as they are by the continuing excellent standard of food and service. Their modern Italian menu holds many delights, but we'd recommend the scaloppine di vitello (escallops of veal with tomato fondue, €24) or one of their legendary steaks, which are so mighty they induce meat sweats in even the most committed carnivore. The average price of dinner for two with a bottle of house wine is about €95, and the thrifty can dine for less with their daily set menu a mere €24 if you eat before 6.45pm, rising to €39.95 for the set dinner menu. So, even if you're not minted, you can still dine alongside the A-list.

- Starters: €7.50-12.50
- Mains: €19-30
- House Wine: €23.95

OPENING: Lunch: Mon-Sun
Dinner: Mon-Sun

**BOOKING:** 662 4800, or book online

# VERRES EN VERS

Golden Lane,
Dublin 8.

www.radissonblu.ie/royalhotel-dublin

**NEW ENTRY**

Located in the Radisson Blu Royal Hotel just off Aungier street, V'n V, or Verres en Vers, is a modern day take on a classic French brasserie, and with its upscale but relaxed atmosphere, it's pulling it off well. A quick scan of the menu reveals staple and classic dishes like steak au poivre (€30.50), salad Nicoise (€20.50) and escargots with garlic and butter (€13.50), but the cool elegance of the place suggests we are a million miles away from rural France. The clean lines, dark wood finishes, recessed bar and subtle floral touches are all complemented by the simple white linen tablecloths and chunky cutlery and crockery, which gives the place a contemporary but relaxed feel that countless restaurants in Dublin try, but fail, to achieve. We'll forgive them the fact that Verres en Ver translates to 'poetry in a glass', which sounds more like a summer ad campaign for cider. We'll also forgive them for the fact that they might be the most difficult restaurant to Google in Dublin – because with food this good in surroundings this pleasant, it's hard to be disappointed with anything about V'n V. The selection of French wines and Champagnes are extensive, as well, and the service is impeccable.

- Starters: €6.50-19
- Mains: €16.95-29.45
- House Wine: €19.50

OPENING: Lunch: Mon-Sun
Dinner: Mon-Sun

**BOOKING:** Tel: 898 2900

# WAGAMAMA

Unit 4B South King St,
Dublin 2.

www.wagamama.ie

This large, bright dining room hasn't changed a bit since it opened in 1998. It is still the canteen of choice for trendy, healthy and upwardly mobile Southsiders. Wagamama claim to be a bastion of "positive eating" whatever that means. Their customers seem to smile a lot while they eat, so they could have a point. The menu features variations of ramen, teriyaki and different types of soups, noodles and, well, noodle soups. Everything is served in a rapid volley by good looking staff who scrawl orders on placemats and seem to be in perpetual motion. The most popular dish here is the chicken katsu curry (€12.75). Many swear by the restorative properties of the chicken ramen, a large bowl of noodles in a pork and chicken soup with menma, spring onions, seasonal greens and a grilled chicken breast. The weekday lunch special offers a main dish and drink for €9.95. We recommend asking for a beef gohan and homemade lemonade. You will speedily be presented by marinated beef strips, courgettes, red onions and mushrooms in an oyster, ginger and garlic sauce served with rice. The bench seating forces customers into close quarters so beware of strangers attempting to chat up your date.

- Starters: €2.65-8.35
- Mains: €10.85-17.30
- House Wine: €18.95

OPENING: Lunch: Mon-Sun
Dinner: Mon-Sun

**BOOKING:** Tel: 478 2152 (Parties of 10+)

# THE WILD GOOSE

1 Sandford Road,
Ranelagh, Dublin 6
*www.thewildgoosegrill.ie*

**NEW ENTRY**

The Ranelagh set had yet another reason to be smug when The Wild Goose opened its doors three years ago. Luxury and comfort are the watchwords at this old-world restaurant, which serves up classic bistro dishes in elegant surroundings. The chargrilled, dry-aged Kettyle steaks (€29) are a particular favourite, while couples often choose the cote de boeuf for two (€100), which is ceremoniously carved at the table. Our money, however, is on the pan-fried goose breast with fresh figs, goose potatoes (roasted in goose fat and toe-curlingly delicious), wild mushrooms, green beans and red wine jus (€26). Or you could watch the funds and plump for the pocket-friendly early bird for roughly the same price: €19.95 for two courses and €24.95 for three courses. The customer service here is equally noteworthy – this is the type of restaurant where they remember your name and wine choice – and hand you back your coat and handbag the next day without so much as a knowing glance. Speaking of which, the Wild Goose is aptly-named. With 400 bins to choose from and the waiting staff's generous approach when serving, well, it makes a visit to this restaurant a little hazy in parts. The food, on the other hand, is utterly memorable.

- Starters: €6-14
- Mains: €17-29
- House Wine: €24

OPENING: Lunch: Sun
Dinner: Tues-Sun

**BOOKING:** Tel: 491 2377, or book online

# THE WINDING STAIR

40 Ormond Quay,
Dublin 1.

www.winding-stair.com

While the quaint little ground floor bookshop has been firmly established as a stalwart of Dublin's literary scene since the 1970s, the Winding Stair upstairs looks well on its way to becoming the same thing for the capital's culinary-minded types. With its windows overlooking the Ha'penny Bridge and the Liffey, it's difficult to imagine a better people-watching spot in Dublin 1 than this upstairs room with its nostalgic ambiance. Couple that with a fantastic Irish seafood chowder with chorizo and treacle bread (€9.95) and you have all the ingredients for a perfect winter afternoon. Since its reincarnation in 2006, The Winding Stair has been serving up Irish cuisine – all of which has been sourced from within the country – with an emphasis on organic produce. If you're heading there in the evening and spot the Irish wild boar, fried spuds, cabbage, black pudding and plum sauce (€20.95) among the specials, consider yourself a very lucky punter. It's a dish that sums up The Winding Stair's typical fair – comforting, quintessentially Irish and perfectly executed. Their wine list is extensive, well laid out and features Dublin's only homegrown wine, Lusca.

- Starters: €5.95-13.95
- Mains: €21.95-26.50
- House Wine: €25

OPENING: Lunch: Mon-Sun
Dinner: Mon-Sun

**BOOKING:** Tel: 872 7320, email: restaurant@winding-stair.com

# YAMAMORI ORIENTAL

12-13 South Great
George's Street, Dublin 2.
www.yamamorientalcafe.ie

**NEW ENTRY**

Emboldened by experience gained seeking out the best restaurants in Dublin, we became the self-appointed culinary pathfinder on a recent stag trip to Liverpool. Misjudging the situation we inadvertently guided our group into the worst Chinese restaurant we've ever visited – think all day buffet, vats of black bean sauce and heat lamps. Oriental cuisine is bastardised in many cities you will visit, reduced to mere takeaway fodder. This is tragic, as good Japanese and Chinese dishes in particular can offer a route to happiness. Thank Buddha for people like Derek Ryan, who has created a veritable riot of flavour in this grand old Dublin setting. With 40 dishes in total, it's best to ask the staff for suggestions, they'll enthusiastically point you in the right direction. We are cheerleaders for the gyoza, steamed and grilled dumplings with a range of fillings like prawn and garlic, tofu or chicken and kimchi priced from €3.50. Partner with a chilled glass of ume shu, a Japanese plum wine (€5). Bewley's Oriental Café opened in this exact spot in 1896 and as the buzzy, intimate atmosphere takes shape, you get the sense there is a little piece of history repeating as another classic dining experience is born.

- Starters: €3.95-6.95
- Mains: €7.95-24.95
- House Wine: €20

OPENING: Lunch: Mon-Sun
Dinner: Mon-Sun

**BOOKING:** Tel: 645 8001

# ZAYTOON

44-45 Camden Street &
14/15 Parliament Street,
Dublin 2.
www.zaytoon.ie

**Z**aytoon has never patronised customers by serving the kind of sub-par offering that other fast food restaurants call a kebab, but which is just a lot of suspect meat (Dog? Cat? Pigeon?) with a bit of limp lettuce and a squirt of the ubiquitous and disconcerting 'Special Sauce' (what on earth is in that, and how long does it remain in one's gut?). Instead they take kebabs seriously, and the result is legendary, not only for their mammoth size, but also for the myriad flavours in each mouthful. It's a rare eatery that you would frequent while enthusiastically drunk, and then return to in the cold harsh light of day for sober dining. But such is the allure of this restaurant, as well as doing a roaring night time trade, is equally busy at lunch and dinner time where their signature barg (fillet of beef marinated in onion and saffron, €11) is quite the favourite. We'd also recommend trying the chicken shish kebab meal (€12), which comes with fries and a soft drink of your choice. This has fuelled our journey home after many the night out, not to mention lined our stomachs in a form of pre-emptive strike on a developing hangover.

● Kebabs €8-13.50

OPENING: Lunch: Mon-Sun
Dinner: Mon-Sun

**BOOKING:** No Reservations

# ALTERNATIVE
## DINING

### CRACKBIRD
*34 South William Street, Dublin 2*

This pop-up restaurant, owned by Joe Macken of Jo'Burger, is named after the "addictive" fried chicken for which it has become renowned. The emphasis at this hipster haven is on sharing (and posing), with huge skillets of buttermilk chicken, made especially for dining *a deux*, and cheaper-by-the-dozen beer deals. If you're partial to poultry, you'll love it.

*For reservations, send them a tweet at twitter.com/ crackBIRDdublin*

### THE PAELLA GUYS
*Markets across Dublin*
*www.facebook.com/thepaellaguys*

The Paella Guys serve authentic paella (€8) and Moorish spiced lamb meatballs (€8) at seven markets around Dublin. Though a relatively recent addition to Dublin's street food offering, they have already scooped the Yellow Tail People's Choice Award at the Dublin Street Food Awards. Quite a handsome bunch of gentlemen as well. Are they on the menu too? We'll get our coats... Find them on Facebook.

### THE DUBLIN FOOD CO-OP
*12 New Market, Dublin 8*
*www.dublinfood.coop/html/markets.html*

Open on Saturday and Sunday, this cafe produces a variety of fare, but it's the 'Amazing Eggs' on brioche that keep the patrons coming back for more. Cooked with cheese, tomato and a whole clove of garlic, these scrambled eggs are arguably the best in the city. The fact that this epicurean delight costs just €4 only adds to the positive vibes.

### PABLO PICANTÉ

*131 Baggot Street and 4*
*Clarendon Market*
*www.pablopicante.ie*

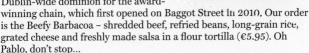

Pablo Picanté's award-winning burritos have gained something of a cult following. In fact, we're predicting Dublin-wide dominion for the award-winning chain, which first opened on Baggot Street in 2010. Our order is the Beefy Barbacoa – shredded beef, refried beans, long-grain rice, grated cheese and freshly made salsa in a flour tortilla (€5.95). Oh Pablo, don't stop...

### POP-UP RESTAURANTS AND SUPPER CLUBS

*Various locations*

If you want a really unique dining experience, check out the new wave of pop-up restaurants and supper clubs that temporarily take over unusual venues in the capital. Enjoy an eight-course tasting menu at the monthly Supper Club Project, *popuprestaurant.ie*; for "Georgian-era opulence", try Faoi Thalamh, which is headed up by Gary Bell, ex-sous chef in Thornton's, *faoithalamh.com* and for good value and good company, try the Sett Club, *settfoodclub.com*

### BOOJUM

*Millennium Walkway,*
*Italian Quarter, Dublin 2*
*boojummex.com/Dublin*

A visit to Boojum goes a little like this: pick a burrito, fajita, burrito bowl or salad, choose a filling and a sauce, and chow down, preferably with an ice-cold *cerveza*. Husband and wife team – and self-confessed "burrito addicts" – John and Karen use authentic imported ingredients, and you can really taste the difference.

# IN THE CITY

# THE 'BURBS

79

BLANCHARDSTOWN

71

PHOENIX PARK

118    INCHICORE

PALMERSTOWN

105    CRU

PARK WEST

16

35

126

28

88

12

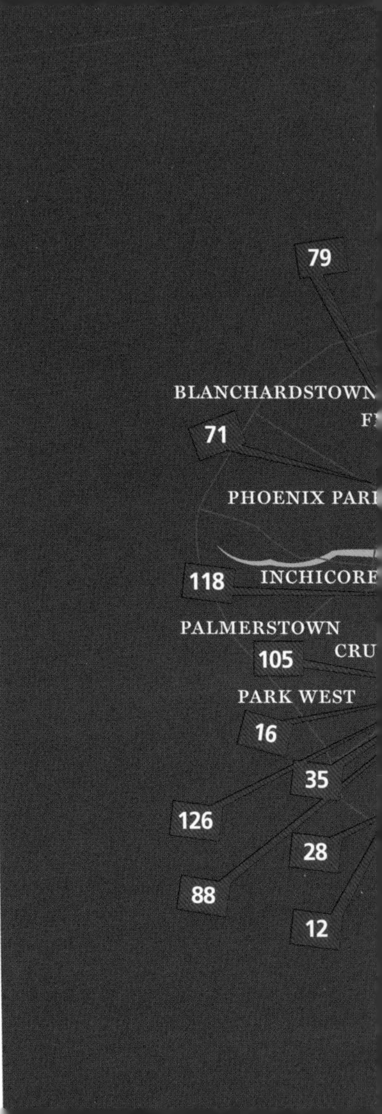

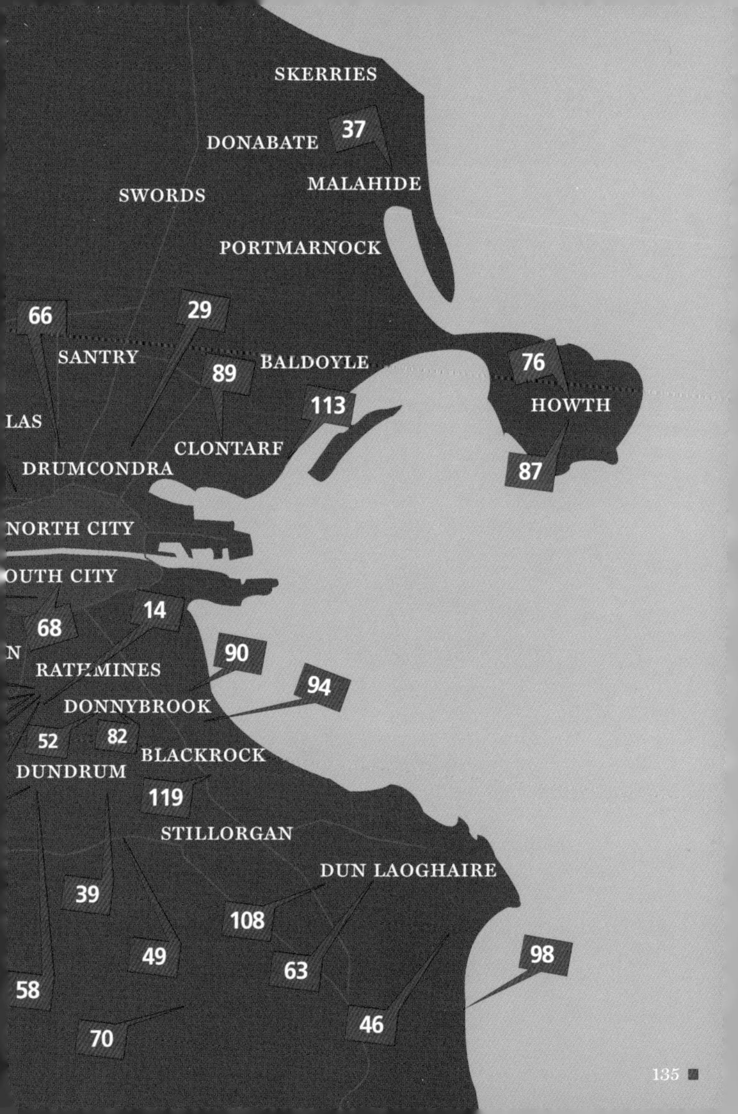

SKERRIES

DONABATE 37

MALAHIDE

SWORDS

PORTMARNOCK

66

29

SANTRY

89 BALDOYLE

113

76

HOWTH

CLONTARF

DRUMCONDRA

87

LAS

NORTH CITY

OUTH CITY

68

14

N

RATHMINES

90

DONNYBROOK

94

52 82

DUNDRUM

BLACKROCK

119

STILLORGAN

DUN LAOGHAIRE

39

108

49

63

98

58

46

70

# WHAT DO YOU
## WANT TO EAT?

# EDITOR'S PICKS

The Port House

We all have different needs each time we dine out in Dublin. Here are our top picks of the best eateries in the city to meet specific needs. Whether you're after a raucous night out with the girls or a more family-friendly affair, these recommendations will point you in the right direction.

**FIRST DATE**

## WINNER: THE PORT HOUSE... 106

Also recommended

**GIRLS' NIGHT OUT**

## WINNER: SABA.................... 8

Also recommended

**BIG NIGHT OUT**

## WINNER: COPPINGER ROW....... 51

Also recommended

**THE 'BURBS**

## WINNER: BON APPETIT ............ 37

Also recommended

**PUSH THE BOAT OUT**

## WINNER: THORNTON'S ...........122

Also recommended

**FAMILY FRIENDLY**

## WINNER: ANDERSONS CREPERIE.. 29

*Also recommended*

| | |
|---|---|
| Wagamama | 125 |
| Lennox Café Bistro | 81 |
| itsa4 | 68 |
| Avoca | 30 |

**BEST VALUE**

## WINNER: LE BON CRUBEEN.......... 38

*Also recommended*

| | |
|---|---|
| Green Nineteen | 62 |
| Louie's | 84 |
| Ouzo's | 98 |
| Paulie's Pizza | 100 |

**CELEBRITY SPOTTING**

## WINNER: TOWN BAR AND GRILL..123

*Also recommended*

| | |
|---|---|
| One Pico | 97 |
| Residence | 110 |
| The Dylan | 55 |
| Marco Pierre White | 85 |

# EDITOR'S
## CHOICE

The Dubliner's *editor,
Martha Connolly, picks
her favourite dishes of
the past year.*

**STARTER:**
Free range
Irish spicy
chicken wings
with Cashel
blue cheese
dip. €8.60,
*McHugh's Wine
and Dine.* P87

**MAIN:**
Roast partridge
with curried
butternut
squash puree,
confit potatoes,
glazed shallots
and a prune jus.
€27, *Dax.* P10

**DESSERT:**
Pistachio macaroon with white chocolate
cream, raspberry jelly and lemon sorbet.
€10.50, *Pearl Brasserie.* P101

Roast partridge with curried
butternut squash puree, confit
potatoes, glazed shallots and
a prune jus.

1. The Bake House
2. The Box Tree
3. Brasserie Le Pont
4. Café Bar H
5. Canal Bank Café
6. Dakshin
7. The Dylan
8. Fallon & Byrne
9. Food Game
10. Good World
11. Hartley's
12. Independent Pizza
13. Itsa4
14. KC Peaches
15. Matt The Thresher
16. McHugh's Wine & Dine
17. Moloughney's of Clontarf
18. Mulberry Garden
19. Noshington
20. O'Connells
21. Oliviers at The Schoolhouse
22. Ouzo's
23. Pacino's
24. The Pig's Ear
25. The Port House
26. Rigby's Deli and Dining Room
27. Seapoint
28. Sean Mac D's
29. The Tea Room at the Clarence
30. Verres en Vers
31. The Wild Goose Grill
32. Yamamori Oriental

1. Alexis
2. Balzac
3. Bang
4. Bar Pintxo
5. Botanic Gardens Restaurant
6. Cornucopia
7. Eden
8. The Exchange
9. Fire Restaurant
10. French Paradox
11. Gruel
12. Herbstreet
13. The House
14. Ivans Oyster Bar and Grill
15. Koh
16. Manifesto
17. Monty's of Kathmandu
18. Ochos
19. The Purty Kitchen
20. The Restaurant
21. Roly's
22. Rotana
23. Salon de Saveurs
24. Il Segreto
25. Taste of Emilia
26. Ukiyo
27. Unicorn
28. Venu
29. Wilde
30. Wolfe's Irish Artisan Bistro

# THE TEN MOST POPULAR RESTAURANTS IN DUBLIN

As voted by readers of *The Dubliner*